SOUTH AFRICA

GOOD STORIES REVEAL as much, or more, about a locale as any map or guidebook. Whereabouts Press is dedicated to publishing books that will enlighten a traveler to the soul of a place. By bringing a country's stories to the English-speaking reader, we hope to convey its culture through literature. Books from Whereabouts Press are essential companions for the curious traveler, and for the person who appreciates how fine writing enhances one's experiences in the world.

"Coming newly into Spanish, I lacked two essentials—a childhood in the language, which I could never acquire, and a sense of its literature, which I could."

—Alastair Reid, *Whereabouts: Notes on Being a Foreigner*

OTHER TRAVELER'S LITERARY COMPANIONS

Amsterdam	*Israel*
Australia	*Italy*
Chile	*Japan*
China	*Mexico*
Costa Rica	*Prague*
Cuba	*Spain*
France	*Vienna*
Greece	*Vietnam*
Ireland	

FORTHCOMING:

Argentina	*India*
Brazil	*Turkey*

SOUTH AFRICA

A TRAVELER'S LITERARY COMPANION

EDITED BY

ISABEL BALSEIRO
AND TOBIAS HECHT

WHEREABOUTS PRESS
BERKELEY, CALIFORNIA

Copyright © 2009 by Whereabouts Press

Preface © 2009 by Isabel Balseiro and Tobias Hecht
(complete copyright information on page 240)

Map of South Africa by BookMatters

Published by
Whereabouts Press
Berkeley, California
www.whereaboutspress.com

Distributed to the trade by PGW / Perseus Distribution

MANUFACTURED IN THE UNITED STATES OF AMERICA

Library of Congress Cataloging-in-Publication Data
South Africa : a traveler's literary companion /
edited by Isabel Balseiro and Tobias Hecht.
p.   cm. — (Travelers literary companions ; 18)
ISBN-13: 978-1-883513-22-1 (alk. paper)
ISBN-10: 1-883513-22-7 (alk. paper)
1. Short stories, South African—Translations into English.
2. South African fiction—21st century—Translations into English.
3. South African—Fiction. I. Balseiro, Isabel. II. Hecht, Tobias.
PQ1278.F68   2008
843'.0108—dc22
2008022099

5   4   3   2   1

Contents

THE RURAL AREAS,
THE FARM, AND THE GAME PARK

In memory of Es'kia Mphahlele

Preface

Whereas travelers may envision journeys geographically, thinking about South African literature through the lens of geography is a Pandora's box. The country's history is about nothing if not the competing interpretations of who has the right to own, settle, name, and exploit the land and its riches. Well before the advent of apartheid, the 1909 Act of Union enshrined in law the virtual impossibility of any political participation by blacks. Then in 1913 the Native's Land Act limited black land ownership to less than ten percent of the country's territory; the least hospitable areas were reserved for Africans. Between these dates, the African Native National Congress (the forerunner to the African National Congress) was founded, initiating a struggle that only in the 1990s would open the way to a democratic society.

The divisions in South Africa involve not only the grand sweep of history but also the micromanagement of space and even of something as ungovernable as desire. Perhaps that is why the chapter included here from Lewis Nkosi's *Mating Birds* presents us with the partition of a single beach into a whites-only area and another to which the narrator—a man longing for a certain woman on the wrong side of the strand—refuses to restrict himself.

The stories and fragments of novels in this book were collected with an eye to evoking a vibrant, enigmatic, and divided South Africa. They were written over the past one hundred years—from just after the Anglo-Boer War (1899–1902) until a decade and a bit after the country's first democratic elections (1994). We have arranged the fiction into four sections: "Gauteng" (which comprises Johannesburg, Pretoria, and nearby areas), "KwaZulu-Natal" (which, with Durban as its largest city, runs along the Indian Ocean and reaches into the vast, overwhelmingly Zulu-speaking countryside), "The Western Cape" (which claims the city of Cape Town as well as some of the country's most fertile farmland), and finally what we call "The Rural Areas, The Farm, and The Game Park."

Debates around location, naming, and landscape abound in South Africa, and geographical references can shift according to language (the country has eleven official languages, English being the mother tongue of less than ten percent of the population). In reading a literature that emerges amid forced migration, rural and urban displacement, involuntary relocation, and legislated land theft, it is natural to wonder how the notions of home, family, movement, forced removal, and employment are imaginatively evoked. For decades, millions of South Africans were forced into a state of perpetual migration within their own country while others went into exile.

The older pieces we have included seem still to resonate in today's South Africa. One of them, Olive Schreiner's

"1899," treats the Anglo-Boer War while another, H. C. Bosman's "The Rooinek," is set in the aftermath of the conflict. Schreiner—the pacifist and firebrand, author of the novel *The Story of an African Farm*—depicts the fate of a line of Afrikaner women in the years leading up to the war and its outbreak, adumbrating a struggle over land that unfurls both backward into the colonial past and forward into the novels of contemporary authors, particularly those of J. M. Coetzee. In "The Rooinek," a derogatory term for a Briton, H. C. Bosman writes about an Englishman who buys a farm among Afrikaners trying to scratch out a living on the land amid the ruins of war. First there is a drought and then an outbreak of anthrax that kills the cows and oxen. With nothing left, the Afrikaners with the rooinek in tow set out on a trek, hoping to reach what was then German South-West Africa, modern-day Namibia. Readers may be taken aback to find that in this piece black people are lifeless shadows referred to by a racist epithet, but even for contemporary black South African authors, Bosman remains a point of reference, seen as a talented oral-style narrator and a master of the short story. Travelers will be intrigued, in any case, by his descriptions of the rugged Marico district and the Kalahari and his portrait of the times.

In "Maiden Outing to Rondebosch," Jan Rabie writes of a brief junket by a group of pioneering ladies ("founders of the nation") led by Jan van Riebeeck, the first Dutch Commander of the Cape, from 1652 to 1662. Venturing part way around the foot of the imposing flat-topped Table Mountain, the group saw "framed in the wild foliage . . .

two brown faces staring open-mouthed." This encounter sets in relief the flashpoints of race and control of the land, with one of the soldiers suggesting—as if hinting at the next 350 years of history—"we only wish to raise food for ourselves."

Who is telling the story and who is representing whom take on enormous significance in South African literature. The form in which the story is recounted is, of course, paramount as well. One piece in this collection, "The Turban," luxuriantly retold by A. C. Jordan, emerges from traditional Xhosa *ntsomi*, a performed narrative genre. Here Jordan has transposed the *ntsomi* into a literary tale that harks back to an uncertain time in the rural, almost mythical, past. The piece is not set in the European form of a folktale; its architecture and aesthetics, while penned for a contemporary readership, incorporate elements of a storytelling that is oral and communal, with symbolism that may be unfamiliar to readers not from Southern Africa.

"The Ultimate Safari" by Nadine Gordimer takes us into something like an inverted safari in which the people migrate, hunt for food, and live in fear of being hunted. The tale is simple in its cruelty and complicated in the geopolitics that frame it. When large tracts of nature like the Kruger National Park were made the playground of whites who sought tame bushveld adventures, Africans were kept out as surely as the animals were kept in. But then again fences aren't impermeable.

Ronnie Govender's story, "1949," concerns the riots between blacks and Indians that convulsed the city of Durban in the middle of the twentieth century. The story is told from an intimate perspective but takes on a conflict as convoluted as it was lethal. Whereas Govender writes of the moment when the match is being dropped into the petrol container, Richard Rive's "Morning 1955" nostalgically and playfully brings to life Cape Town's District Six, the community lost forever with the forced removal of 60,000 people of color following the 1966 declaration that this was to be a white area. District Six and Goodwood in Cape Town, Cato Manor in Durban, Sophiatown in Johannesburg, and many other communities across the country fell victim to the draconian urban segregation policies put into effect through the enforcement of the 1950 Group Areas Act.

While some are forcibly removed, others simply have difficulty being at home in their homes. Ivan Vladislavić's minimalist piece, "The Alarmed House," evokes the bane and salve of contemporary urban life in South Africa, burglar alarms. Under the lonely glow of the keypad, an unease with the city attends the comings and goings of a people seemingly in thrall to the device's impertinent beeps. A sometimes invisible underside belies the postcard-perfect image of Cape Town. *Krot*, by Rustum Kozain, offers a glimpse into the shutting mind of a man whose life becomes inextricably bound to the house he inhabits. Caught in a losing battle against the passage of time, both house and man fall into decay and solitude despite occasional encounters with an external world whose very liveliness awakens resentment.

Ahmed Essop takes us into the Johannesburg suburb of Fordsburg, which the apartheid government designated for people of Indian descent. Racial, religious, and familial tensions emerge when a dying man wishes to return to the

Muslim home of his brother after decades of self-imposed estrangement from his community.

South Africa is a land of contrasts, with standards of living ranging from miserable to mink, where late-model BMWs speed past hungry children. As thousands die every week from AIDS, Britons fly in for bypass surgery, avoiding the long delays at home, and affluent women book package tours that combine plastic surgery with safaris (during downtime). The landscapes evoked in this book (from the Indian Ocean to the stark villages of the Eastern Cape, from the leafy suburbs of Johannesburg to the parched hinterlands of the Northern Cape) will no doubt pique the interest of the traveler. But then in a number of the pieces the setting is partially overshadowed by the focus on human relations, as if social life were itself the setting. Es'kia Mphahlele's "Mrs. Plum," a gem of twentieth-century South African prose, takes place mostly in a Johannesburg suburb. But Johannesburg is almost incidental because, more than in a city, the tale is set in the strife between a white liberal "madam," or lady of the house, and the black domestic worker. It is a story recounted from the perspective of someone not credited with the means to articulate her thoughts but nevertheless capable of laying bare her white liberal employer's bootless protest against a system that in many ways suits her. As with the geographical setting, violence is peripheral to the story—at first glance; but where dogs eat better than the woman who scrubs the toilets or the man who tends the garden, the understated brutality permeates everything. In this long short story, Mphahlele captures that brutality, but with a mordant humor.

Zachariah Rapola's "Street Features" evokes an avenue in Johannesburg where everything happens: couples mate, children fly kites, drunkards brawl, prostitutes stroll, pickpockets steal, and the homeless seek refuge. Palesa, a prostitute and "weaver of words," captures the narrator's attention, but after he becomes infatuated with the woman he is unable to disentangle her from the structure of the place. Like Hieronymus Bosch's painting "The Garden of Earthly Delights," where men emerge from shells and animals torture humans, Rapola's writing is lush with a vitality of things and the decay of people.

There was a lot to choose from for this book, which made our task by turns easy and very difficult, easy because we almost couldn't go wrong in selecting works from certain authors, difficult because there was limited space and the collection required internal coherence. In the end we included what we regard as examples of the most probing and provocative South African literature, pieces that we hope will give readers a sense of the country—its landscapes, history, and social life—and tempt them to read on.

For their suggestions and comments, we warmly thank Gabeba Baderoon, Brenda Cooper, Heidi Grunebaum, Rustum Kozain, Ntongela Masilela, Roshila Nair, Zachariah Rapola, and Mark Sanders. The Centre for African Studies at the University of Cape Town was an ideal setting to begin work on this book, while Derek Gowlett and Kobus Steyn offered invaluable help with translations. The Alexander and Adelaide Hixon Professorship provided sabbatical support. For their research assistance we are grateful to Andrew Leverentz and Maureen de Lourdes Ruiz. We also wish to thank our publisher David Peattie for his nimble work in bringing out this book.

Isabel Balseiro and Tobias Hecht

The Alarmed House

Ivan Vladislavić

I

WHEN A HOUSE HAS BEEN ALARMED, it becomes explosive. It must be armed and disarmed several times a day. When it is armed, by the touching of keys upon a pad, it emits a whine that sends the occupants rushing out, banging the door behind them. There are no leisurely departures: there is no time for second thoughts, for taking a scarf from the hook behind the door, for checking that the answering machine is on, for a final look in the mirror on the way through the hallway. There are no savored homecomings either: you do not unwind into such a house, kicking off your shoes, breathing the familiar air. Every departure is precipitate, every arrival is a scraping-in.

IVAN VLADISLAVIĆ (1957–) is the author of five books of fiction and the eclectic *Portrait with Keys* (from which this excerpt is taken), about life in Johannesburg. He has won some of South Africa's top literary awards, including the *Sunday Times* Literary Prize and the Alan Paton Award. An accomplished editor, he has worked with many of South Africa's major writers.

In an alarmed house, you awake in the small hours to find the room unnaturally light. The keys on the touch pad are aglow with a luminous, clinical green, like a night-light for a child who's afraid of the dark.

Mrs. Plum

Es'kia Mphahlele

MY MADAM'S NAME was Mrs. Plum. She loved dogs and Africans and said that everyone must follow the law even if it hurt. These were three big things in Madam's life.

I came to work for Mrs. Plum in Greenside, not very far from the center of Johannesburg, after leaving two white families. The first white people I worked for as a cook and laundry woman were a man and his wife in Parktown North. They drank too much and always forgot to pay me. After five months I said to myself, No. I am going to leave these drunks. So that was it. That day I was as angry as a red-hot iron when it meets water. The second house I cooked and washed for had five children who were badly brought up. This was in Belgravia. Many times they called me You Black Girl and I kept quiet. Because their mother heard them and said nothing. Also I was only new from

ES'KIA MPHAHLELE (1919–2008). Trained as a teacher, he was jailed in 1952 for his opposition to the discriminatory Bantu Education system. In 1957 he began a twenty-year period of exile. A major figure in African literature, he is best known for his autobiography *Down Second Avenue* and the novel *The Wanderers*. The story "Mrs. Plum" is abridged here.

Phokeng my home, far away near Rustenburg, I wanted to learn and know the white people before I knew how far to go with the others I would work for afterward. The thing that drove me mad and made me pack and go was a man who came to visit them often. They said he was a cousin or something like that. He came to the kitchen many times and tried to make me laugh. He patted me on the buttocks. I told the master. The man did it again and I asked the madam that very day to give me my money and let me go.

These were the first nine months after I had left Phokeng to work in Johannesburg. There were many of us girls and young women from Phokeng, from Zeerust, from Shuping, from Kosten, and many other places who came to work in the cities. So the suburbs were full of blackness. Most of us had already passed Standard Six and so we learned more English where we worked. None of us likes to work for white farmers, because we know too much about them on the farms near our homes. They do not pay well and they are cruel people.

At Easter time so many of us went home for a long weekend to see our people and to eat chicken and sour milk and *morogo*—wild spinach. We also took home sugar and condensed milk and tea and coffee and sweets and custard powder and tinned foods.

It was a home-girl of mine, Chimane, who called me to take a job in Mrs. Plum's house, just next door to where she worked. This is the third year now. I have been quite happy with Mrs. Plum and her daughter Kate. By this I mean that my place as a servant in Greenside is not as bad as that of many others. Chimane too does not complain much. We are paid six pounds a month with free food and free servant's room. No one can ever say that they are well paid, so we go on complaining somehow. Whenever we meet on Thursday afternoons, which is time off for all of us black women in the suburbs, we talk and talk and talk: about our people at home and their letters; about their illnesses; about bad crops; about a sister who wanted a school uniform and books and school fees; about some of our madams and masters who are good, or stingy with money or food, or stupid, or full of nonsense, or who kill themselves and each other, or who are dirty—and so many things I cannot count them all.

Thursday afternoons we go to town to look at the shops, to attend a women's club, to see our boyfriends, to go to bioscope some of us. We turn up smart, to show others the clothes we bought from the black men who sell soft goods to servants in the suburbs. We take a number of things and they come round every month for a bit of money until we finish paying. Then we dress the way of many white madams and girls. I think we look really smart. Sometimes we catch the eyes of a white woman looking at us and we laugh and laugh and laugh until we nearly drop on the ground because we feel good inside ourselves.

II

What did the girl next door call you? Mrs. Plum asked me the first day I came to her. Jane, I replied. Was there not an African name? I said yes, Karabo. All right, Madam said. We'll call you Karabo, she said. She spoke as if she knew a name is a big thing. I knew so many whites who did not care what they called black people as long as it was all right for their tongue. This pleased me, I mean

Mrs. Plum's use of *Karabo;* because the only time I heard the name was when I was at home or when my friends spoke to me. Then she showed me what to do: meals, meal times, washing, and where all the things were that I was going to use.

My daughter will be here in the evening, Madam said. She is at school. When the daughter came, she added, she would tell me some of the things she wanted me to do for her every day.

Chimane, my friend next door, had told me about the daughter Kate, how wild she seemed to be, and about Mr. Plum who had killed himself with a gun in a house down the street. They had left the house and come to this one.

Madam is a tall woman. Not slender, not fat. She moves slowly, and speaks slowly. Her face looks very wise; her forehead seems to tell me she has a strong liver: she is not afraid of anything. Her eyes are always swollen at the lower eyelids like a white person who has not slept for many many nights or like a large frog. Perhaps it is because she smokes too much, like wet wood that will not know whether to go up in flames or stop burning. She looks me straight in the eyes when she talks to me, and I know she does this with other people too. At first this made me fear her, now I am used to her. She is not a lazy woman, and she does many things outside, in the city and in the suburbs.

This was the first thing her daughter Kate told me when she came and we met. Don't mind mother, Kate told me. She said, She is sometimes mad with people for very small things. She will soon be all right and speak nicely to you again.

Kate, I like her very much, and she likes me too. She tells me many things a white woman does not tell a black servant. I mean things about what she likes and does not like, what her mother does or does not do, all these. At first I was unhappy and wanted to stop her, but now I do not mind.

Kate looks very much like her mother in the face. I think her shoulders will be just as round and strong-looking. She moves faster than Madam. I asked her why she was still at school when she was so big. She laughed. Then she tried to tell me that the school where she was was for big people, who had finished with lower school. She was learning big things about cooking and food. She can explain better, me I cannot. She came home on weekends.

Since I came to work for Mrs. Plum Kate has been teaching me plenty of cooking. I first learned from her and Madam the word *recipes*. When Kate was at the big school, Madam taught me how to read cookery books. I went on very slowly at first, slower than an ox-wagon. Now I know more. When Kate came home, she found I had read the recipe she left me. So we just cooked straightaway. Kate thinks I am fit to cook in a hotel. Madam thinks so too. Never never! I thought. Cooking in a hotel is like feeding oxen. No one can say thank you to you. After a few months I could cook the Sunday lunch and later I could cook specials for Madam's or Kate's guests.

Madam did not only teach me cooking. She taught me how to look after guests. She praised me when I did very very well; not like the white people I had worked for before. I do not know what runs crooked in the heads of other people. Madam also had classes in the evenings for servants to teach them how to read and write. She and two other women in Greenside taught in a church hall.

As I say, Kate tells me plenty of things about Madam. She says to me she says, My mother goes to meetings many times. I ask her I say, What for? She says to me she says, For your people. I ask her I say, My people are in Phokeng far away. They have got mouths, I say. Why does she want to say something for them? Does she know what my mother and what my father want to say? They can speak when they want to. Kate raises her shoulders and drops them and says, How can I tell you Karabo? I don't say your people—your family only, I mean all the black people in this country. I say, Oh! What do the black people want to say? Again she raises her shoulders and drops them, taking a deep breath.

I ask her I say, With whom is she in the meeting?

She says, With other people who think like her.

I ask her I say, Do you say there are people in the world who think the same things?

She nods her head.

I ask, What things?

So that a few of your people should one day be among those who rule this country, get more money for what they do for the white man, and—what did Kate say again? Yes, that Madam and those who think like her also wanted my people who have been to school to choose those who must speak for them in the—I think she said it looks like a *Kgotla* at home who rule the villages.

I say to Kate I say, Oh I see now. I say, Tell me Kate why is Madam always writing on the machine, all the time every day nearly?

She replies she says, Oh my mother is writing books.

I ask, You mean a book like those? pointing at the books on the shelves.

Yes, Kate says.

And she told me how Madam wrote books and other things for newspapers and she wrote for the newspapers and magazines to say things for the black people who should be treated well, be paid more money, for the black people who can read and write many things to choose those who want to speak for them.

Kate also told me she said, My mother and other women who think like her put on black belts over their shoulders when they are sad and they want to show the white government they do not like the things being done by whites to blacks. My mother and the others go and stand where the people in government are going to enter or go out of a building.

I ask her I say, Does the government and the white people listen and stop their sins? She says, No. But my mother is in another group of white people.

I ask, Do the people of the government give the women tea and cakes? Kate says, Karabo! How stupid . . . oh!

I say to her I say, Among my people if someone comes and stands in front of my house I tell him to come in and I give him food. You white people are wonderful. But they keep standing there and the government people do not give them anything.

She replies, You mean strange. How many times have I taught you not to say *wonderful* when you mean *strange!* Well, Kate says with a short heart and looking cross and she shouts, Well they do not stand there the whole day to ask for tea and cakes stupid. Oh dear!

Always when Madam finished to read her newspapers she gave them to me to read to help me speak and write better English. When I had read she asked me to tell her some of the things in it. In this way, I did better and better and my mind was opening and opening and I was learning and learning many things about the black people inside and outside the towns which I did not know in the least. When I found words that were too difficult or I did not understand some of the things I asked Madam. She always told me, You see this, you see that, eh? with a heart that can carry on a long way. Yes, Madam writes many letters to the papers. She is always sore about the way the white police beat up black people; about the way black people who work for whites are made to sit at the Zoo Lake with their hearts hanging, because the white people say our people are making noise on Sunday afternoon when they want to rest in their houses and gardens; about many ugly things that happen when some white people meet black men on the pavement or street. So Madam writes to the papers to let others know, to ask the government to be kind to us.

In the first year Mrs. Plum wanted me to eat at table with her. It was very hard, one because I was not used to eating at table with a fork and knife, two because I heard of no other kitchen worker who was handled like this. I was afraid. Afraid of everybody, of Madam's guests if they found me doing this. Madam said I must not be silly. I must show that African servants can also eat at table. Number three, I could not eat some of the things I loved very much: mealie-meal porridge with sour milk or *morogo*, stamped mealies mixed with butter beans, sour porridge for breakfast, and other things. Also, except for morning porridge, our food is nice when you eat with the hand. So nice that it does not stop in the mouth or the throat to greet anyone before it passes smoothly down.

We often had lunch together with Chimane next door and our garden boy—Ha! I must remember never to say *boy* again when I talk about a man. This makes me think of a day during the first few weeks in Mrs. Plum's house. I was talking about Dick her garden man and I said "garden boy." And she says to me she says, Stop talking about a "boy," Karabo. Now listen here, she says, You Africans must learn to speak properly about each other. And she says, White people won't talk kindly about you if you look down upon each other.

I say to her I say, Madam, I learned the word from the white people I worked for, and all the kitchen maids say "boy."

She replies she says to me, Those are white people who know nothing, just low-class whites. I say to her I say, I thought white people know everything.

She said, You'll learn my girl and you must start in this house, hear? She left me there thinking, my mind mixed up.

I learned. I grew up.

III

If any woman or girl does not know the Black Crow Club in Bree Street, she does not know anything. I think nearly everything takes place inside and outside that house. It is just where the dirty part of the City begins, with factories and the market. After the market is the place where Indi-

ans and Colored people live. It is also at the Black Crow
that the buses turn round and back to the black townships.
Noise, noise, noise all the time. There are women who sell
hot sweet potatoes and fruit and monkey nuts and boiled
eggs in the winter, boiled mealies and the other things
in the summer, all these on the pavements. The streets
are always full of potato and fruit skins and monkey nut
shells. There is always a strong smell of roast pork. I think
it is because of Piel's cold storage down Bree Street.

Madam said she knew the black people who work in
the Black Crow. She was happy that I was spending my
afternoon on Thursdays in such a club. You will learn sewing, knitting, she said, and other things that you like. Do
you like to dance? I told her I said, Yes, I want to learn.
She paid the two shillings fee for me each month.

We waited on the first floor, we the ones who were
learning sewing, waiting for the teacher. We talked
and laughed about madams and masters, and their children and their dogs and birds and whispered about our
boyfriends.

Sies! My Madam you do not know—*mojuta oa'nete*—a
real miser . . .

Jo—jo—jo! You should see our new dog. A big thing
like this. People! Big in a foolish way . . .

What! Me, I take a master's bitch by the leg, me, and
throw it away so that it keeps howling, *tjwe, tjwe! Ngo—
wu ngo—wu!* I don't play about with them, me . . .

Shame, poor thing! God sees you, true. . . !

They wanted me to take their dog out for a walk every
afternoon and I told them I said, It is not my work in
other houses the garden man does it. I just said to myself

I said, they can go to the chickens. Let them bite their elbow before I take out a dog, I am not so mad yet . . .

Hei! It is not like the child of my white people who keeps a big white rat and you know what? He puts it on his bed when he goes to school. And let the blankets just begin to smell of urine and all the nonsense and they tell me to wash them. *Hei,* people!

Did you hear about Rebone, people? Her Madam put her out, because her master was always tapping her buttocks with his fingers. And yesterday the madam saw the master press Rebone against himself . . .

Jo—jo—jo! People!

Dirty white man!

No, not dirty. The madam smells too old for him.

Hei! Go and wash your mouth with soap, this girl's mouth is dirty . . .

Jo, Rebone, daughter of the people! We must help her to find a job before she thinks of going back home.

The teacher came. A woman with strong legs, a strong face, and kind eyes. She had short hair and dressed in a simple but lovely floral frock. She stood well on her legs and hips. She had a black mark between the two top front teeth. She smiled as if we were her children. Our group began with games, and then Lilian Ngoyi took us for sewing. After this she gave a brief talk to all of us from the different classes.

I can never forget the things this woman said and how she put them to us. She told us that the time had passed for black girls and women in the suburbs to be satisfied with working, sending money to our people and going to see them once a year. We were to learn, she said, that the world would never be safe for black people until they were in the government with the power to make laws. The power should be given by the Africans who were more than the whites.

We asked her questions and she answered them with wisdom. I shall put some of them down in my own words as I remember them.

Shall we take the place of the white people in the government?

Some yes. But we shall be more than they as we are more in the country. But also the people of all colors will come together and there are good white men we can choose and there are Africans some white people will choose to be in the government.

There are good madams and masters and bad ones. Should we take the good ones for friends?

A master and a servant can never be friends. Never, so put that out of your head, will you! You are not even sure if the ones you say are good are not like that because they cannot breathe or live without the work of your hands. As long as you need their money, face them with respect. But you must know that many sad things are happening in our country and you, all of you, must always be learning, adding to what you already know, and obey us when we ask you to help us.

At other times Lilian Ngoyi told us she said, Remember your poor people at home and the way in which the whites are moving them from place to place like sheep and cattle. And at other times again she told us she said, Remember that a hand cannot wash itself—it needs another to do it.

I always thought of Madam when Lilian Ngoyi spoke.

I asked myself, What would she say if she knew that I was listening to such words. Words like: A white man is looked after by his black nanny and his mother when he is a baby. When he grows up the white government looks after him, sends him to school, makes it impossible for him to suffer from the great hunger, keeps a job ready and open for him as soon as he wants to leave school. Now Lilian Ngoyi asked she said, How many white people can be born in a white hospital, grow up in white streets, be clothed in lovely cotton, lie on white cushions; how many whites can live all their lives in a fenced place away from people of other colors and then, as men and women learn quickly the correct ways of thinking, learn quickly to ask questions in their minds, big questions that will throw over all the nice things of a white man's life? How many? Very very few! For those whites who have not begun to ask, it is too late. For those who have begun and are joining us with both feet in our house, we can only say Welcome!

I was learning. I was growing up. Every time I thought of Madam, she became more and more like a dark forest which one fears to enter, and which one will never know. But there were several times when I thought, This woman is easy to understand, she is like all other white women.

What else are they teaching you at the Black Crow, Karabo?

I tell her I say, Nothing, Madam. I ask her I say, Why does Madam ask?

You are changing.

What does Madam mean?

Well, you are changing.

But we are always changing, Madam.

And she left me standing in the kitchen. This was a few days after I had told her that I did not want to read more than one white paper a day. The only magazines I wanted to read, I said to her, were those from overseas, if she had them. I told her that white papers had pictures of white people most of the time. They talked mostly about white people and their gardens, dogs, weddings, and parties. I asked her if she could buy me a Sunday paper that spoke about my people. Madam bought it for me. I did not think she would do it.

There were mornings when, after hanging the white people's washing on the line, Chimane and I stole a little time to stand at the fence and talk. We always stood where we could be hidden by our rooms.

Hei, Karabo, you know what? That was Chimane.

No, what? Before you start, tell me, has Timi come back to you?

Ach, I do not care. He is still angry. But boys are fools—they always come back dragging themselves on their empty bellies. *Hei* you know what?

Yes?

The Thursday past I saw Moruti K.K. I laughed until I dropped on the ground. He is standing in front of the Black Crow. I believe his big stomach was crying from hunger. Now he has a small dog in his armpit, and is standing before a woman selling boiled eggs and—*hei* home-girl!—tripe and intestines are boiling in a pot—oh, the smell! You could fill a hungry belly with it, the way it was good. I think Moruti K.K. is waiting for the woman to buy a boiled egg. I do not know what the woman was still doing. I am standing nearby. The dog keeps wriggling and pushing out its nose, looking at the boiling tripe. Moruti keeps patting it with his free hand, not so? Again the dog wants to spill out of Moruti's hand and it gives a few sounds through the nose. *Hei* man, home-girl! One two three the dog spills out to catch some of the good meat! It misses falling into the hot gravy in which the tripe is swimming I do not know how. Moruti K.K. tries to chase it. It has tumbled onto the women's eggs and potatoes and all are in the dust. She stands up and goes after K.K. She is shouting to him to pay, not so? Where am I at that time? I am nearly dead with laughter the tears are coming down so far.

I was myself holding tight on the fence so as not to fall through laughing. I held my stomach to keep back a pain in the side.

I ask her I say, Did Moruti K.K. come back to pay for the wasted food?

Yes, he paid.

The dog?

He caught it. That is a good African dog. A dog must look for its own food when it is not time for meals. Not these stupid spoiled angels the whites keep giving tea and biscuits.

Hmm.

Dick our garden man joined us, as he often did. When the story was repeated to him the man nearly rolled on the ground laughing.

He asks, Who is Reverend K.K.?

I say, He is the owner of the Black Crow.

Oh!

We reminded each other, Chimane and I, of the round minister. He would come into the club, look at us with a smooth smile on his smooth round face. He would look at each one of us, with that smile on all the time, as if he had forgotten that it was there. Perhaps he had, because as he looked at us, almost stripping us naked with his watery shining eyes—funny—he could have been a farmer looking at his ripe corn, thinking many things.

K.K. often spoke without shame about what he called ripe girls—*matjitjana*—with good firm breasts. He said such girls were pure without any nonsense in their heads and bodies. Everybody talked a great deal about him and what they thought he must be doing in his office whenever he called in so-and-so.

The Reverend K.K. did not belong to any church. He baptized, married, and buried people for a fee, who had no church to do such things for them. They said he had been driven out of the Presbyterian Church. He had formed his own, but it did not go far. Then he later came and opened the Black Crow. He knew just how far to go with Lilian Ngoyi. She said although she used his club to teach us things that would help us in life, she could not go on if he was doing any wicked things with the girls in his office. Moruti K.K. feared her, and kept his place.

IV

When I began to tell my story I thought I was going to tell you mostly about Mrs. Plum's two dogs. But I have been talking about people. I think Dick is right when he says, What is a dog! And there are so many dogs cats and parrots in Greenside and other places that Mrs. Plum's dogs do not look special. But there was something special in the dog business in Madam's house. The way in which she loved them, maybe.

Monty is a tiny animal with long hair and small black eyes and a face nearly like that of an old woman. The other, Malan, is a bit bigger, with brown and white colors. It has small hair and looks naked by the side of the friend. They sleep in two separate baskets which stay in Madam's bedroom. They are to be washed often and brushed and sprayed and they sleep on pink linen. Monty has a pink ribbon which stays on his neck most of the time. They both carry a cover on their backs. They make me fed up when I see them in their baskets, looking fat, and as if they knew all that was going on everywhere.

It was Dick's work to look after Monty and Malan, to feed them, and to do everything for them. He did this together with garden work and cleaning of the house. He came at the beginning of this year. He just came, as if from nowhere, and Madam gave him the job as she had chased away two before him, she told me. In both those cases, she said that they could not look after Monty and Malan.

Dick had a long heart, even though he told me and Chimane that European dogs were stupid, spoiled. He said, One day those white people will put earrings and toe rings and bangles on their dogs. That would be the day he would leave Mrs. Plum. For, he said, he was sure that she would want him to polish the rings and bangles with Brasso.

Although he had a long heart, Madam was still not sure of him. She often went to the dogs after a meal or after a cleaning and said to them, Did Dick give you food sweethearts? Or, Did Dick wash you sweethearts? Let me see. And I could see that Dick was blowing up like a balloon with anger. These things called white people! he said to me. Talking to dogs!

I say to him I say, People talk to oxen at home do I not say so?

Yes, he says, but at home do you not know that a man speaks to an ox because he wants to make it pull the plough or the wagon or to stop or to stand still for a person to inspan it. No one simply goes to an ox looking at him with eyes far apart and speaks to it. Let me ask you, do you ever see a person where we come from take a cow and press it to his stomach or his cheek? Tell me!

And I say to Dick I say, We were talking about an ox, not a cow.

He laughed with his broad mouth until tears came out of his eyes. At a certain point I laughed aloud too.

One day when you have time, Dick says to me, he says, you should look into Madam's bedroom when she has put a notice outside her door.

Dick, what are you saying? I ask.

I do not talk, me. I know deep inside me.

Dick was about our age, I and Chimane. So we always said *moshiman'o* when we spoke about his tricks. Because he was not too big to be a boy to us. He also said to us, *Hei, lona banyana kelona*—Hey you girls, you! His large mouth always seemed to be making ready to laugh. I think Madam did not like this. Many times she would say, What is there to make you laugh here? Or in the garden she would say, This is a flower and when it wants water that is not funny! Or again, If you did more work and stopped trying to water my plants with your smile you would be more useful. Even when Dick did not mean to smile. What Madam did not get tired of saying was, If I left you to look after my dogs without anyone to look after you at the same time you would drown the poor things.

Dick smiled at Mrs. Plum. Dick hurt Mrs. Plum's dogs? Then cows can fly. He was really, really afraid of white people, Dick. I think he tried very hard not to feel afraid. For he was always showing me and Chimane in private how Mrs. Plum walked and spoke. He took two bowls and pressed them to his chest, speaking softly to them as Madam speaks to Monty and Malan. Or he sat at Madam's table and acted the way she sits when writing. Now and again he looked back over his shoulder, pulled his face long like a horse's making as if he were looking over his glasses while telling me something to do. Then he would sit on one of the armchairs, cross his legs, and act the way Madam drank her tea; he held the cup he was thinking about between his thumb and the pointing finger, only letting their nails meet. And he laughed after every act. He did these things, of course, when Madam was not home. And where was I at such times? Almost flat on my stomach, laughing.

But oh how Dick trembled when Mrs. Plum scolded him! He did his housecleaning very well. Whatever mistake he made, it was mostly with the dogs: their linen, their food. One white man came into the house one afternoon to tell Madam that Dick had been very careless when taking the dogs out for a walk. His own dog was waiting on Madam's stoep. He repeated that he had been driving down our street; and Dick had let loose Monty and Malan to cross the street. The white man made plenty of noise about this and I think wanted to let Madam know how useful he had been. He kept on saying, Just one inch, *just* one inch. It was lucky I put on my brakes quick enough . . . But your boy kept on smiling—why? Strange. My boy would only do it twice and only twice and then . . . ! His pass. The man moved his hand like one writing, to mean that he would sign his servant's pass for him to go and never come back. When he left, the white man said, Come on Rusty, the boy is waiting to clean you. Dogs with names, men without, I thought.

Madam climbed on top of Dick for this, as we say.

Once one of the dogs, I don't know which—Malan or Monty—took my stocking—brand new, you hear—and tore it with its teeth and paws. When I told Madam about it, my anger as high as my throat, she gave me money to buy another pair. It happened again. This time she said she was not going to give me money because I must also keep my stockings where the two gentlemen would not reach them. Mrs. Plum did not want us ever to say *Voetsek* when we wanted the dogs to go away. Me I said this when they came sniffing at my legs or fingers. I hate it.

In my third year in Mrs. Plum's house, many things happened, most of them all bad for her. There was trouble with Kate; Chimane had big trouble; my heart was twisted by two loves; and Monty and Malan became real dogs for a few days.

Madam had a number of suppers and parties. She invited Africans to some of them. Kate told me the reasons for some of the parties. Like her mother's books when finished, a visitor from across the seas, and so on. I did not like the black people who came here to drink and eat. They spoke such difficult English like people who were full of all the books in the world. They looked at me as if I were right down there whom they thought little of—me a black person like them.

One day I heard Kate speak to her mother. She says I don't know why you ask so many Africans to the house. A few will do at a time. She said something about the government which I could not hear well. Madam replies she says to her, You know some of them do not meet white people often, so far away in their dark houses. And she says to Kate that they do not come because they want her as a friend but they just want a drink for nothing.

I simply felt that I could not be the servant of white people and of blacks at the same time. At my home or in my room I could serve them without a feeling of shame. And now, if they were only coming to drink!

But one of the black men and his sister always came to the kitchen to talk to me. I must have looked unfriendly the first time, for Kate talked to me about it afterward as she was in the kitchen when they came. I know that at that time I was not easy at all. I was ashamed and I felt that a white person's house was not the place for me to look happy in front of other black people while the white man looked on.

Another time it was easier. The man was alone. I shall never forget that night, as long as I live. He spoke kind words and I felt my heart grow big inside me. It caused me to tremble. There were several other visits. I knew that

I loved him, I could never know what he really thought of me, I mean as a woman and he as a man. But I loved him, and I still think of him with a sore heart. Slowly I came to know the pain of it. Because he was a doctor and so full of knowledge and English I could not reach him. So I knew he could not stoop down to see me as someone who wanted him to love me.

Kate turned very wild. Mrs. Plum was very much worried. Suddenly it looked as if she were a new person, with new ways and new everything. I do not know what was wrong or right. She began to play the big gramophone aloud, as if the music were for the whole of Greenside. The music was wild and she twisted her waist all the time, with her mouth half open. She did the same things in her room. She left the big school and every Saturday night now she went out. When I looked at her face, there was something deep and wild there on it, and when I thought she looked young she looked old, and when I thought she looked old she was young. We were both 22 years of age. I think that I could see the reason why her mother was so worried, why she was suffering.

Worse was to come.

They were now openly screaming at each other. They began in the sitting room and went upstairs together, speaking fast hot biting words, some of which I did not grasp. One day Madam comes to me and says, You know Kate loves an African, you know the doctor who comes to supper here often. She says he loves her too and they will leave the country and marry outside. Tell me, Karabo, what do your people think of this kind of thing between a white woman and a black man? It *cannot* be right is it?

I reply and I say to her, We have never seen it happen before where I come from.

That's right, Karabo, it is just madness.

Madam left. She looked like a hunted person.

These white women, I say to myself I say, these white women, why do not they love their own men and leave us to love ours!

From that minute I knew that I would never want to speak to Kate. She appeared to me as a thief, as a fox that falls upon a flock of sheep at night. I hated her. To make it worse, he would never be allowed to come to the house again.

Whenever she was home there was silence between us. I no longer wanted to know anything about what she was doing, where or how.

I lay awake for hours on my bed. Lying like that, I seemed to feel parts of my body beat and throb inside me, the way I have seen big machines doing, pounding and pounding and pushing and pulling and pouring some water into one hole which came out at another end. I stretched myself so many times so as to feel tired and sleepy.

When I did sleep, my dreams were full of painful things.

One evening I made up my mind, after putting it off many times. I told my boyfriend that I did not want him any longer. He looked hurt, and that hurt me too. He left.

The thought of the African doctor was still with me and it pained me to know that I should never see him again, unless I met him in the street on a Thursday afternoon. But he had a car. Even if I did meet him by luck, how could I make him see that I loved him? Ach, I do not believe he would even stop to think what kind of woman I am. Part of that winter was a time of longing and burning for me. I say part because there are always things to keep servants busy whose white people go to the sea for the winter.

To tell the truth, winter was the time for servants, not nannies, because they went with their madams so as to look after the children. Those like me stayed behind to look after the house and dogs. In winter so many families went away that the dogs remained the masters and madams. You could see them walk like white people in the streets. Silent but with plenty of power. And when you saw them you knew that they were full of more nonsense and fancies in the house.

There was so little work to do.

One week word was whispered round that a home-boy of ours was going to hold a party in his room on Saturday. I think we all took it for a joke. How could the man be so bold and stupid? The police were always driving about at night looking for black people; and if the whites next door heard the party noise—*oho*! But still, we were full of joy and wanted to go. As for Dick, he opened his big mouth and nearly fainted when he heard of it and that I was really going.

During the day on the big Saturday Kate came.

She seemed a little less wild. But I was not ready to talk to her. I was surprised to hear myself answer her when she said to me, Mother says you do not like a marriage between a white girl and a black man, Karabo.

Then she was silent.

She says, But I want to help him, Karabo.

I ask her I say, You want to help him to do what?

To go higher and higher, to the top.

I knew I wanted to say so much that was boiling in my chest. I could not say it. I thought of Lilian Ngoyi at the Black Crow, what she said to us. But I was mixed up in my head and in my blood.

You still agree with my mother?

All I could say was, I said to your mother I had never seen a black man and a white woman marrying, you hear me? What I think about it is my business.

I remembered that I wanted to iron my party dress and so I left her. My mind was full of the party again and I was glad because Kate and the doctor would not worry my peace that day. And the next day the sun would shine for all of us, Kate or no Kate, doctor or no doctor.

The house where our home-boy worked was hidden from the main road by a number of trees. But although we asked a number of questions and counted many fingers of bad luck until we had no more hands for fingers, we put on our best pay-while-you-wear dresses and suits and clothes bought from boys who had stolen them, and went to our home-boy's party. We whispered all the way while we climbed up to the house. Someone who knew told us that the white people next door were away for the winter. Oh, so that is the thing! we said.

We poured into the garden through the back and stood in front of his room laughing quietly. He came from the big house behind us, and were we not struck dumb when he told us to go into the the white people's house! Was he mad? We walked in with slow footsteps that seemed to be sniffing at the floor, not sure of anything. Soon we were standing and sitting all over on the nice warm cushions and the heaters were on. Our home-boy turned the lights low. I counted fifteen people inside. We saw how we loved one another's evening dress. The boys were smart too.

Our home-boy's girlfriend Naomi was busy in the kitchen preparing food. He took out glasses and cold drinks—fruit juice, tomato juice, ginger beers, and so many other kinds of soft drink. It was just too nice. The tarts, the biscuits, the snacks, the cakes, *woo*, that was a party, I tell you. I think I ate more ginger cake than I had ever done in my life. Naomi had baked some of the things. Our home-boy came to me and said I do not want the police to come here and have reason to arrest us, so I am not serving hot drinks, not even beer. There is no law that we cannot have parties, is there? So we can feel free. Our use of this house is the master's business. If I had asked him he would have thought me mad.

I say to him I say, You have a strong liver to do such a thing.

He laughed.

He played pennywhistle music on gramophone records—Miriam Makeba, Dorothy Masuka, and other African singers and players. We danced and the party became more and more noisy and more happy. *Hai*, those girls Miriam and Dorothy, they can sing, I tell you! We ate more and laughed more and told more stories. In the middle of the party, our home-boy called us to listen to what he was going to say. Then he told us how he and a friend of his in Orlando collected money to bet on a horse for the July Handicap in Durban. They did this each year but lost. Now they had won two hundred pounds. We all clapped hands and cheered. Two hundred pounds—*woo!*

You should go and sit at home and just eat time, I say to him. He laughs and says, You have no understanding not one little bit.

To all of us he says, Now my brothers and sisters enjoy yourselves. At home I should slaughter a goat for us to feast and thank our ancestors. But this is town life and we must thank them with tea and cake and all those sweet things. I know some people think I must be so bold that I could be midwife to a lion that is giving birth, but enjoy yourselves and have no fear.

Madam came back looking strong and fresh.

The very week she arrived the police had begun again to search servants' rooms. They were looking for what they called loafers and men without passes who they said were living with friends in the suburbs against the law. Our dog's meat boys became scarce because of the police. A boy who had a girlfriend in the kitchens, as we say, always told his friends that he was coming for dog's meat when he meant he was visiting his girl. This was because we gave our boyfriends part of the meat the white people bought for the dogs and us.

One night a white and a black policeman entered Mrs. Plum's yard. They said they had come to search. She says, No, they cannot. They say, Yes, they must do it. She answers, No. They forced their way to the back, to Dick's room and mine. Mrs. Plum took the hose that was running in the front garden and quickly went round to the back. I cut across the floor to see what she was going to say to the men. They were talking to Dick, using dirty words. Mrs. Plum did not wait; she just pointed the hose at the two policemen. This seemed to surprise them. They turned round and she pointed it into their faces. Without their seeing me I went to the tap at the corner of the house and opened it more. I could see Dick, like me, was trying to keep down his laughter. They shouted and tried to wave the water away, but she kept the hose pointing at them, now moving it up and down. They turned and ran through the back gate, swearing the while.

That fixes them, Mrs. Plum said.

The next day the morning paper reported it.

They arrived in the afternoon—the two policemen—with another. They pointed out Mrs. Plum and she was led to the police station. They took her away to answer for stopping the police while they were doing their work.

She came back and said she had paid bail.

At the magistrate's court, Madam was told that she had done a bad thing. She would have to pay a fine or else go to prison for fourteen days. She said she would go to jail to show that she felt she was not in the wrong.

Kate came and tried to tell her that she was doing something silly going to jail for a small thing like that. She tells Madam she says, This is not even a thing to take to the high court. Pay the money. What is £5?

Madam went to jail.

She looked very sad when she came out. I thought of what Lilian Ngoyi often said to us: You must be ready to go to jail for the things you believe are true and for which you are taken by the police. What did Mrs. Plum really believe about me, Chimane, Dick, and all the other black people? I asked myself. I did not know. But from all those things she was writing for the papers and all those meetings she was going to where white people talked about black people and the way they are treated by the government, from what those white women with black bands over their shoulders were doing standing where a white government man was going to pass, I said to myself I said, This woman, *hai*, I do not know she seems to think very much of us black people. But why was she so sad?

Kate came back home to stay after this. She still played the big gramophone loud-loud-loud and twisted her body at her waist until I thought it was going to break. Then I saw a young white man come often to see her. I watched them through the opening near the hinges of the door between the kitchen and the sitting room where they sat. I saw them kiss each other for a long long time. I saw him lift up Kate's dress and her white-white legs begin to tremble, and—oh I am afraid to say more, my heart was beating hard. She called him Jim. I thought it was funny because white people in the shops call black men Jim.

Kate had begun to play with Jim when I met a boy who loved me and I loved. He was much stronger than the one I sent away and I loved him more, much more. The face of the doctor came to my mind often, but it did not hurt me so any more. I stopped looking at Kate and her Jim through openings. We spoke to each other, Kate and I, almost as freely as before but not quite. She and her mother were friends again.

Hallo, Karabo, I heard Chimane call me one morning as I was starching my apron. I answered. I went to the line to hang it. I saw she was standing at the fence, so I knew she had something to tell me. I went to her.

Hallo!

Hallo, Chimane!

O kae?

Ke teng. Wena?

At that moment a woman came out through the back door of the house where Chimane was working.

I have not seen that one before, I say, pointing with my head.

Chimane looked back. Oh, that one. *Hei*, daughter-of-the-people, *Hei*, you have not seen miracles. You know this is Madam's mother-in-law as you see her there. Did I never tell you about her?

No, never.

White people, nonsense. You know what? That poor woman is here now for two days. She has to cook for herself and I cook for the family.

On the same stove?

Yes, She comes after me when I have finished.

She has her own food to cook?

Yes, Karabo. White people have no heart no sense.

What will eat them up if they share their food?

Ask me, just ask me. God! She clapped her hands to show that only God knew, and it was His business, not ours.

Chimane asks me she says, Have you heard from home?

I tell her I say, Oh daughter-of-the-people, more and more deaths. Something is finishing the people at home. My mother has written. She says they are all right, my father too and my sisters, except for the people who have

died. Malebo, the one who lived alone in the house I
showed you last year, a white house, he is gone. Then
teacher Sedimo. He was very thin and looked sick all the
time. He taught my sisters not me. His mother-in-law you
remember I told you died last year—no, the year before.
Mother says also there is a woman she does not think I
remember because I last saw her when I was a small girl
she passed away in Zeerust she was my mother's greatest
friend when they were girls. She would have gone to her
burial if it was not because she has swollen feet.

How are the feet?

She says they are still giving her trouble. I ask Chimane, How are your people at Nokaneng? They have not
written?

She shook her head.

I could see from her eyes that her mind was on another
thing and not her people at that moment.

Wait for me Chimane eh, forgive me, I have scones
in the oven, eh! I will just take them out and come back,
eh!

When I came back to her Chimane was wiping her
eyes. They were wet.

Karabo, you know what?

E—e. I shook my head.

I am heavy with child.

Hau!

There was a moment of silence.

Who is it, Chimane?

Timi. He came back only to give me this.

But he loves you. What does he say; have you told him?

I told him yesterday. We met in town.

I remembered I had not seen her at the Black Crow.

Are you sure, Chimane? You have missed a month?

She nodded her head.

Timi himself—he did not use the thing?

I only saw after he finished, that he had not.

Why? What does he say?

He tells me he says, I should not worry I can be his wife.

Timi is a good boy, Chimane. How many of these boys with town ways who know too much will even say, Yes it is my child?

Hai, Karabo, you are telling me other things now. Do you not see that I have not worked long enough for my people? If I marry now who will look after them when I am the only child?

Hm. I hear your words. It is true. I tried to think of something soothing to say.

Then I say, You can talk it over with Timi. You can go home and when the child is born you look after it for three months and when you are married you come to town to work and can put your money together to help the old people while they are looking after the child.

What shall we be eating all the time I am at home? It is not like those days gone past when we had land and our mother could go to the fields until the child was ready to arrive.

The light goes out in my mind and I cannot think of the right answer. How many times have I feared the same thing! Luck and the mercy of the gods that is all I live by. That is all we live by—all of us.

. . .

Thursday came, and the afternoon off. At the Black Crow I did not see Chimane. I wondered about her. In the evening I found a note under my door. It told me if Chimane was not back that evening I should know that she was at 660 3rd Avenue, Alexandra Township. I was not to tell the white people.

I asked Dick if he could not go to Alexandra with me after I had washed the dishes. At first he was unwilling. But I said to him I said, Chimane will not believe that you refused to come with me when she sees me alone. He agreed.

On the bus Dick told me much about his younger sister whom he was helping with money to stay at school until she finished, so that she could become a nurse and a midwife. He was very fond of her, as far as I could find out. He said he prayed always that he should not lose his job, as he had done many times before, after staying a few weeks only at each job. Because of this he had to borrow monies from people to pay his sister's school fees, to buy her clothes and books. He spoke of her as if she were his sweetheart. She was clever at school, pretty (she was this in the photo Dick had shown me before). She was in Orlando Township. She looked after his old people, although she was only thirteen years of age. He said to me he said, Today I still owe many people because I keep losing my job. You must try to stay with Mrs. Plum, I said.

I cannot say that I had all my mind on what Dick was telling me. I was thinking of Chimane: what could she be doing? Why that note?

We found her in bed. In that terrible township where night and day are full of knives and bicycle chains and guns and the barking of hungry dogs and of people in trouble. I held my heart in my hands. She was in pain and her face, even in the candlelight, was gray. She turned her eyes at me. A fat woman was sitting in a chair. One arm rested on the other and held her chin in its palm. She had hardly opened the door for us after we had shouted our names when she was on her bench again as if there were nothing else to do.

She snorted, as if to let us know that she was going to speak. She said, There is your friend. There she is my own-own niece who comes from the womb of my own sister, my sister who was made to spit out my mother's breast to give way for me. Why does she go and do such an evil thing. *Ao*! You young girls of today you do not know children die so fast these days that you have to thank God for sowing a seed in your womb to grow into a child. If she had let the child be born I should have looked after it or my sister would have been so happy to hold a grandchild on her lap, but what does it help? She has allowed a worm to cut the roots, I don't know.

Then I saw that Chimane's aunt was crying. Not once did she mention her niece by her name, so sore her heart must have been. Chimane only moaned.

Her aunt continued to talk, as if she was never going to stop for breath, until her voice seemed to move behind me, not one of the things I was thinking: trying to remember signs, however small, that could tell me more about this moment in a dim little room in a cruel township without streetlights, near Chimane. Then I remembered the three-legged cat, its gray-green eyes, its *meow*. What was this shadow that seemed to walk about us but was not coming right in front of us?

I thanked the gods when Chimane came to work at the end of the week. She still looked weak, but that shadow was no longer there. I wondered why Chimane had never told me about her aunt before. Even now I did not ask her.

I told her I told her white people that she was ill and had been fetched to Nokaneng by a brother. They would never try to find out. They seldom did, these people. Give them any lie, and it will do. For they seldom believe you whatever you say. And how can a black person work for white people and be afraid to tell them lies? They are always asking the questions, you are always the one to give the answers.

Chimane told me all about it. She had gone to a woman who did these things. Her way was to hold a sharp needle, cover the point with the finger, and guide it into the womb. She then fumbled in the womb until she found the egg and then pierced it. She gave you something to ease the bleeding. But the pain, spirits of our forefathers!

Mrs. Plum and Kate were talking about dogs one evening at dinner. Every time I brought something to table I tried to catch their words. Kate seemed to find it funny, because she laughed aloud. There was a word I could not hear well which began with *sem*—: whatever it was, it was to be for dogs. This I understood by putting a few words together. Mrs. Plum said it was something that was common in the big cities of America, like New York. It was also something Mrs. Plum wanted and Kate laughed at the thought. Then later I was to hear that Monty and Malan could be sure of a nice burial.

Chimane's voice came up to me in my room the next morning, across the fence. When I come out she tells me she says, *Hei* child-of-my-father, here is something to tickle your ears. You know what? What? I say. She says, These white people can do things that make the gods angry. More godless people I have not seen. The madam of our house says the people of Greenside want to buy ground where they can bury their dogs. I heard them talk about it in the sitting room when I was giving them coffee last night. *Hei*, people, let our forefathers come and save us!

Yes, I say, I also heard the madam of our house talk about it with her daughter. I just heard it in pieces. By my mother one day these dogs will sit at table and use knife and fork. These things are to be treated like people now, like children who are never going to grow up.

Chimane sighed and she says, *Hela batho*, why do they not give me some of that money they will spend on the ground and on gravestones to buy stockings! I have nothing to put on, by my mother.

Over her shoulder I saw the cat with three legs.

I pointed with my head. When Chimane looked back and saw it she said, *Hm*, even *they* live like kings. The mother-in-law found it on a chair and the madam said the woman should not drive it away. And there was no other chair, so the woman went to her room.

Hela!

I was going to leave when I remembered what I wanted to tell Chimane. It was that five of us had collected £1 each to lend her so that she could pay the woman of Alexandra for having done that thing for her. When Chimane's time came to receive money we collected each month and which we took in turns, she would pay us back. We were ten women and each gave £2 at a time. So one waited ten months to receive £20. Chimane thanked us for helping her.

I went to wake up Mrs. Plum as she had asked me. She was sleeping late this morning. I was going to knock at the door when I heard strange noises in the bedroom. What is the matter with Mrs. Plum? I asked myself. Should I call her, in case she is ill? No, the noises were not those of a sick person. They were happy noises but like those a person makes in a dream, the voice full of sleep. I bent a little to peep through the keyhole. What is this? I kept asking myself. Mrs. Plum! Malan! What is she doing this one? Her arm was round Malan's belly and pressing its back against her stomach at the navel, Mrs. Plum's body in a nightdress moving in jerks like someone in fits . . . her leg rising and falling . . . Malan silent like a thing to be owned without any choice it can make to belong to another.

The gods save me! I heard myself saying, the words sounding like wind rushing out of my mouth. So this is what Dick said I would find out for myself!

No one could say where it all started, who talked about it first, whether the police wanted to make a reason for taking people without passes and people living with servants and working in town or not working at all. But the story rushed through Johannesburg that servants were going to poison the white people's dogs. Because they were too much work for us: that was the reason. We heard that letters were sent to the newspapers by white people asking the police to watch over the dogs to stop any wicked things. Some said that we the servants were not really bad; we were being made to think of doing these things by evil people in town and in the locations. Others said the police should watch out lest we poison madams and masters because black people did not know right from wrong when they were angry. We were still children at heart, others said. Mrs. Plum said that she had also written to the papers.

Then it was the police came down on the suburbs like locusts on a cornfield. There were lines and lines of men who were arrested hour by hour in the day. They liked this very much, the police. Everybody they took, everybody who was working was asked, Where's the poison eh? Where did you hide it? Who told you to poison the dogs eh? If you tell us we'll leave you to go free, you hear? and so many other things.

Dick kept saying, It is wrong this thing they want to do to kill poor dogs. What have these things of God done to be killed for? Is it the dogs that make us carry passes? Is it dogs that make the laws that give us pain? People are just mad they do not know what they want, stupid! But when white policeman spoke to him, Dick trembled and lost his tongue and the things he thought. He just shook his head. A few moments after they had gone through his pockets he still held his arms stretched out, like the man of straw who frightens away birds in a field. Only when I hissed and gave him a sign did he drop his arms. He rushed to a corner of the garden to go on with his work.

Mrs. Plum had put Monty and Malan in the sitting room, next to her. She looked very much worried. She called me. She asked me she said, Karabo, you think Dick is a boy we can trust? I did not know how to answer. I did not know whom she was talking about when she said *we*. Then I said I do not know, Madam. You know! she said. I looked at her. I said, I do not know what Madam thinks. She said she did not think anything; that was why she asked. I nearly laughed because she was telling a lie this time and not I.

At another time I should have been angry if she lied to me, perhaps. She and I often told each other lies, as Kate and I also did. Like when she came back from jail, after that day when she turned a hosepipe on two policemen. She said life had been good in jail. And yet I could see she was ashamed to have been there. Not like our black people who are always being put in jail and only look at it as the white man's evil game. Lilian Ngoyi often told us this, and Mrs. Plum showed me how true those words are. I am sure that we have kept to each other by lying to each other.

There was something in Mrs. Plum's face as she was speaking which made me fear her and pity her at the same time. I had seen her when she had come from prison; I had seen her when she was shouting at Kate and the girl left the house; now there was this thing about dog poisoning. But never had I seen her face like this before. The eyes, the nostrils, the lips, the teeth seemed to be full of hate, tired, fixed on doing something bad; and yet there was something on that face that told me she wanted me on her side.

Dick is all right, Madam, I found myself saying. She took Malan and Monty in her arms and pressed them to herself, running her hands over their heads. They looked so safe, like a child in a mother's arm.

Mrs. Plum said, All right you may go. She said, Do not tell anybody what I have asked about Dick eh?

When I told Dick about it, he seemed worried.

It is nothing, I told him.

I had been thinking before that I did not stand with those who wanted to poison the dogs, Dick said. But the police have come out. I do not care what happens to the dumb things, now.

I asked him I said, Would you poison them if you were told by someone to do it?

No. But I do not care, he replied.

The police came again and again. They were having a good holiday, everyone could see that. A day later Mrs. Plum told Dick to go because she would not need his work any more.

Dick was almost crying when he left. Is madam so unsure of me? he asked. I never thought a white person could fear me! And he left.

Chimane shouted from the other yard. She said, *Hei ngoana'rona*, the boers are fire-hot eh!

Mrs. Plum said she would hire a man after the trouble was over.

A letter came from my parents in Phokeng. In it they told me my uncle had passed away. He was my mother's brother. The letter also told me of other deaths. They said I would not remember some, I was sure to know the others. There were also names of sick people.

I went to Mrs. Plum to ask her if I could go home. She asks she says, When did he die? I answer I say, It is three days, Madam. She says, So that they have buried him? I reply, Yes Madam. Why do you want to go home then? Because my uncle loved me very much, Madam. But what are you going to do there? To take my tears and words of grief to his grave and to my old aunt, madam. No you cannot go, Karabo. You are working for me you know? Yes, Madam. I, and not your people pay you. I must go Madam, that is how we do it among my people, Madam. She paused. She walked into the kitchen and came out again. If you want to go, Karabo, you must lose the money for the days you will be away. Lose my pay, Madam? Yes, Karabo.

The next day I went to Mrs. Plum and told her I was leaving for Phokeng and was not coming back to her. Could she give me a letter to say that I worked for her. She did, with her lips shut tight. I could feel that something between us was burning like raw chilies. The letter simply said that I had worked for Mrs. Plum for three years. Nothing more. The memory of Dick being sent away was still an open sore in my heart.

The night before the day I left, Chimane came to see me in my room. She had her own story to tell me. Timi, her boyfriend, had left her—for good. Why? Because I killed his baby. Had he not agreed that you should do it? No. Did he show he was worried when you told him you were heavy? He was worried, like me as you saw me, Karabo. Now he says if I kill one I shall eat all his children up when we are married. You think he means what he says? Yes, Karabo. He says his parents would have been very happy to know that the woman he was going to marry can make his seed grow.

Chimane was crying, softly.

I tried to speak to her, to tell her that if Timi left her just like that, he had not wanted to marry her in the first place. But I could not, no, I could not. All I could say was, Do not cry, my sister, do not cry. I gave her my handkerchief.

Kate came back the morning I was leaving, from somewhere very far I cannot remember where. Her mother took no notice of what Kate said asking her to keep me, and I was not interested either.

One hour later I was on the Railway bus to Phokeng. During the early part of the journey I did not feel anything about the Greenside house I had worked in. I was not really myself, my thoughts dancing between Mrs. Plum, my uncle, my parents, and Phokeng, my home. I slept and woke up many times during the bus ride. Right through the ride I seemed to see, sometimes in sleep, sometimes between sleep and waking, a red car passing our bus, then running behind us. Each time I looked out it was not there.

Dreams came and passed. He tells me he says, You have killed my seed I wanted my mother to know you are a woman in whom my seed can grow . . . Before you make the police take you to jail make sure that it is for something big you should go to jail for, otherwise you will come out with a heart and mind that will bleed inside you and poison you . . .

The bus stopped for a short while, which made me wake up.

The Black Crow, the club women . . . *Hei*, listen! I lie

to the madam of our house and I say I had a telegram from my mother telling me she is very very sick. I show her a telegram my sister sent me as if mother were writing. So I went home for a nice weekend . . .

The laughter of the women woke me up, just in time for me to stop a line of saliva coming out over my lower lip. The bus was making plenty of dust now as it was running over part of the road they were digging up. I was sure the red car was just behind us, but it was not there when I woke.

Any one of you here who wants to be baptized or has a relative without a church who needs to be can come and see me in the office . . . A round man with a fat tummy and sharp hungry eyes, a smile that goes a long, long way . . .

The bus was going uphill, heavily and noisily.

I kick a white man's dog, me, or throw it there if it has not been told the black people's law . . . This is Mister Monty and this is Mister Malan. Now get up you lazy boys and meet Mister Kate. Hold out your hands and say hallo to him . . . Karabo, bring two glasses there . . . Wait a bit—What will you chew boys while Mister Kate and I have a drink? Nothing? Sure?

We were now going nicely on a straight tarred road and the trees rushed back. Mister Kate. What nonsense, I thought.

Look Karabo, madam's dogs are dead. What? Poison. I killed them. She drove me out of a job did she not? For nothing. Now I want her to feel she drove me out for something. I came back when you were in your room and took the things and poisoned them . . . And you know what? She has buried them in clean pink sheets in the garden. *Ao,* clean clean good sheets. I am going to dig them out and take one sheet do you want the other one? Yes, give me the other one I will send it to my mother . . . *Hei,* Karabo, see here they come. Monty and Malan. The bloody fools they do not want to stay in their hole. Go back you silly fools. Oh you do not want to move eh? Come here, now I am going to throw you in the big pool. No, Dick! No Dick! No, no! Dick! They cannot speak do not kill things that cannot speak. Madam can speak for them she always does. No! Dick . . . !

I woke up with a jump after I had screamed Dick's name, almost hitting the window. My forehead was full of sweat. The red car also shot out of my sleep and was gone. I remembered a friend of ours who told us how she and the garden man had saved two white sheets in which their white master had buried their two dogs. They went to throw the dogs in a dam.

When I told my parents my story Father says to me he says, So long as you are in good health my child, it is good. The worker dies, work does not. There is always work. I know when I was a boy a strong sound body and a good mind were the biggest things in life. Work was always there, and the lazy man could never say there was no work. But today people see work as something bigger than everything else, bigger than health, because of money.

I reply I say, Those days are gone Papa. I must go back to the city after resting a little to look for work. I must look after you. Today people are too poor to be able to help you.

I knew when I left Greenside that I was going to return to Johannesburg to work. Money was little, but life was full and it was better than sitting in Phokeng and watching the sun rise and set. So I told Chimane to keep her eyes and ears open for a job.

I had been at Phokeng for one week when a red car arrived. Somebody was sitting in front with the driver, a white woman. At once I knew it to be that of Mrs. Plum. The man sitting beside her was showing her the way, for he pointed toward our house in front of which I was sitting. My heart missed a few beats. Both came out of the car. The white woman said "Thank you" to the man after he had spoken a few words to me.

I did not know what to do and how to look at her as she spoke to me. So I looked at the piece of cloth I was sewing pictures on. There was a tired but soft smile on her face.

The Hajji

Ahmed Essop

WHEN THE TELEPHONE RANG several times one evening and his wife did not attend to it as she usually did, Hajji Hassen, seated on a settee in the lounge, cross-legged and sipping tea, shouted, "Salima, are you deaf?" And when he received no response from his wife and the jarring bell went on ringing, he shouted again, "Salima, what's happened to you?"

The telephone stopped ringing. Hajji Hassen frowned in a contemplative manner, wondering where his wife was now. Since his return from Mecca after the pilgrimage, he had discovered novel inadequacies in her, or perhaps saw the old ones in a more revealing light. One of her salient inadequacies was never to be around when he wanted her. She was either across the road confabulating with her sister, or gossiping with the neighbors, or away on a shopping spree. And now, when the telephone had gone

AHMED ESSOP (1931–) was born in India and went to South Africa as a child. He taught English at schools in Johannesburg. An author of short stories, novels, and poetry, he won the Olive Schreiner Award for *The Hajji and Other Stories* (1978). "The Hajji" is slightly abridged here.

on assaulting his ears, she was not in the house. He took another sip of the strongly spiced tea to stifle the irritation within him.

When he heard the kitchen door open he knew that Salima had entered. The telephone burst out again in a metallic shrill and the Hajji shouted for his wife. She hurried to the phone.

"Hullo . . . Yes . . . Hassen . . . Speak to him? . . . Who speaking? . . . Caterine? . . . Who Caterine? . . . Au-right . . . I call him."

She put the receiver down gingerly and informed her husband in Gujarati that a woman named "Caterine" wanted to speak to him. The name evoked no immediate association in his memory. He descended from the settee and squeezing his feet into a pair of crimson sandals, went to the telephone.

"Hullo . . . Who? . . . Catherine? . . . No, I don't know you . . . Yes . . . Yes . . . Oh . . . now I remember . . . Yes . . ."

He listened intently to the voice, urgent, supplicating. Then he gave his answer:

"I am afraid I can't help him. Let the Christians bury him. His last wish means nothing to me . . . Madam, it's impossible . . . No . . . Let him die . . . Brother? Pig! Pig! Bastard!" He banged the receiver onto the telephone in explosive annoyance.

"O Allah!" Salima exclaimed. "What words! What is this all about?"

He did not answer but returned to the settee, and she quietly went to the bedroom.

Salima went to bed and it was almost midnight when

her husband came into the room. His earlier vexation had now given place to gloom. He told her of his brother Karim who lay dying in Hillbrow. Karim had cut himself off from his family and friends ten years ago; he had crossed the color line (his fair complexion and gray eyes serving as passports) and gone to cohabit with a white woman. And now that he was on the verge of death he wished to return to the world he had forsaken and to be buried under Muslim funeral rites and in a Muslim cemetery.

Hajji Hassen had, of course, rejected the plea, and for good reason. When his brother had crossed the color line, he had severed his family ties. The Hajji at that time had felt excoriating humiliation. By going over to the white Herrenvolk, his brother had trampled on something that was vitally part of him, his dignity and self-respect. But the rejection of his brother's plea involved a straining of the heartstrings and the Hajji did not feel happy. He had recently sought God's pardon for his sins in Mecca, and now this business of his brother's final earthly wish and his own intransigence was in some way staining his spirit.

The next day Hassen rose at five to go to the mosque. When he stepped out of his house in Newtown the street-lights were beginning to pale and clusters of houses to assume definition. The atmosphere was fresh and heady, and he took a few deep breaths. The first trams were beginning to pass through Bree Street and were clanging along like decrepit yet burning specters toward the Johannesburg City Hall. Here and there a figure moved along hurriedly. The Hindu fruit and vegetable hawkers were starting up their old trucks in the yards, preparing to go out for the day to sell to suburban housewives.

When he reached the mosque the Somali muezzin in the ivory-domed minaret began to intone the call for prayers. After prayers, he remained behind to read the Koran in the company of two other men. When he had done, the sun was shining brilliantly in the courtyard onto the flowers and the fountain with its goldfish.

Outside the house he saw a car. Salima opened the door and whispered, "Caterine." For a moment he felt irritated, but realizing that he might as well face her, he stepped boldly into the lounge.

Catherine was a small woman with firm fleshy legs. She was seated cross-legged on the settee, smoking a cigarette. Her face was almost boyish, a look that partly originated in her auburn hair which was cut very short, and partly in the smallness of her head. Her eyebrows, firmly penciled, accentuated the gray-green glitter of her eyes. She was dressed in a dark gray costume.

He nodded his head at her to signify that he knew who she was. Over the telephone he had spoken with aggressive authority. Now, in the presence of the woman herself, he felt a weakening of his masculine fiber.

"You must, Mr. Hassen, come to see your brother."

"I am afraid I am unable to help," he said in a tentative tone. He felt uncomfortable; there was something so positive and intrepid about her appearance.

"He wants to see you. It's his final wish."

"I have not seen him for ten years."

"Time can't wipe out the fact that he's your brother."

"He is a white. We live in different worlds."

"But you must see him."

There was a moment of strained silence.

"Please understand that he's not to blame for having broken with you. I am to blame. I got him to break with you. Really you must blame me, not Karim."

Hassen found himself unable to say anything. The thought that she could in some way have been responsible for his brother's rejection of him had never occurred to him. He looked at his feet in awkward silence. He could only state in a lazily recalcitrant tone, "It is not easy for me to see him."

"Please come, Mr. Hassen, for my sake, please. I'll never be able to bear it if Karim dies unhappily. Can't you find it in your heart to forgive him, and to forgive me?"

He could not look at her. A sob escaped from her, and he heard her opening her handbag for a handkerchief.

"He's dying. He wants to see you for the last time."

Hassen softened. He was overcome by the argument that she had been responsible for taking Karim away. He could hardly look on her responsibility as being in any way culpable. She was a woman.

"If you remember the days of your youth, the time you spent together with Karim before I came to separate him from you, it will be easier for you to pardon him."

Hassen was silent.

"Please understand that I am not a racialist. You know the conditions in this country."

He thought for a moment and then said, "I will go with you."

He excused himself and went to his room to change. After a while they set off for Hillbrow in her car.

He sat beside her. The closeness of her presence, the perfume she exuded stirred currents of feeling within him. He glanced at her several times, watched the deft movements of her hands and legs as she controlled the car. Her powdered profile, the outline taut with a resolute quality, aroused his imagination. There was something so businesslike in her attitude and bearing, so involved in reality (at the back of his mind there was Salima—flaccid, cowlike, and inadequate) that he could hardly refrain from expressing his admiration.

"You must understand that I'm only going to see my brother because you have come to me. For no one else would I have changed my mind."

"Yes, I understand. I'm very grateful."

"My friends and relatives are going to accuse me of softness, of weakness."

"Don't think of them now. You have decided to be kind to me."

The realism and the common sense of the woman's words! He was overwhelmed by her.

The car stopped at the entrance of a building in Hillbrow. They took the lift. On the second floor three white youths entered and were surprised at seeing Hassen. There was a separate lift for non-whites. They squeezed themselves into a corner, one actually turning his head away with a grunt of disgust. The lift reached the fifth floor too soon for Hassen to give a thought to the attitude of the three white boys. Catherine led him to apartment 65.

He stepped into the lounge. Everything seemed to be

carefully arranged. There was her personal touch about the furniture, the ornaments, the paintings. She went to the bedroom, then returned and asked him in.

Karim lay in bed, pale, emaciated, his eyes closed. For a moment Hassen failed to recognize him: ten years divided them. Catherine placed a chair next to the bed for him. He looked at his brother and again saw, through ravages of illness, the familiar features. She sat on the bed and rubbed Karim's hands to wake him. After a while he began to show signs of consciousness. She called him tenderly by his name. When he opened his eyes he did not recognize the man beside him, but by degrees, after she had repeated Hassen's name several times, he seemed to understand. He stretched out a hand and Hassen took it, moist and repellent. Nausea swept over him, but he could not withdraw his hand as his brother clutched it firmly.

"Brother Hassen, please take me away from here."

Hassen's agreement brought a smile to his lips.

Catherine suggested that she drive Hassen back to Newtown where he could make preparations to transfer Karim to his home.

"No, you stay here. I will take a taxi." And he left the apartment.

In the corridor he pressed the button for the lift. He watched the indicator numbers succeeding each other rapidly, then stop at five. The doors opened—and there they were again, the three white youths. He hesitated. The boys looked at him tauntingly. Then suddenly they burst into deliberately brutish laughter.

"Come into the parlor," one of them said.

"Come into the Indian parlor," another said in a cloyingly mocking voice.

Hassen looked at them, annoyed, hurt. Then something snapped within him and he stood there, transfixed. They laughed at him in a raucous chorus as the lift doors shut.

He remained immobile, his dignity clawed. Was there anything so vile in him that the youths found it necessary to maul that recess of self-respect within him? "They are whites," he said to himself in bitter justification of their attitude.

He would take the stairs and walk down the five floors. As he descended he thought of Karim. Because of him he had come there and because of him he had been insulted. The enormity of the insult bridged the gap of ten years when Karim had spurned him, and diminished his being. Now he was diminished again.

He was hardly aware that he had gone down five floors when he reached ground level. He stood still, expecting to see the three youths again. But the foyer was empty and he could see the reassuring activity of street life through the glass panels. He quickly walked out as though he would regain in the hubbub of the street something of his assaulted dignity.

He walked on, structures of concrete and glass on either side of him, and it did not even occur to him to take a taxi. It was in Hillbrow that Karim had lived with the white woman and forgotten the existence of his brother; and now that he was dying he had sent for him. For ten years Karim had lived without him. O Karim! The thought of the youth he had loved so much during the days they had been together at the Islamic Institute, a religious seminary though it was governed like a penitentiary, brought the tears to his eyes and he stopped against a shop window and wept. A few pedestrians looked at him. When the shopkeeper came outside to see the weeping man, Hassen, ashamed of himself, wiped his eyes and walked on.

He regretted his pliability in the presence of the white woman. She had come unexpectedly and had disarmed him with her presence and subtle talk. A painful lump rose in his throat as he set his heart against forgiving Karim. If his brother had had no personal dignity in sheltering behind his white skin, trying to be what he was not, he was not going to allow his own moral worth to be depreciated in any way.

When he reached central Johannesburg he went to the station and took the train. In the coach with the blacks he felt at ease and regained his self-possession. He was among familiar faces, among people who respected him. He felt as though he had been spirited away by a perfumed well-made wax doll, but had managed with a prodigious effort to shake her off.

When he reached home Salima asked him what had been decided and he answered curtly, "Nothing." But feeling elated after his escape from Hillbrow he added condescendingly, "Karim left of his own accord. We should have nothing to do with him."

Salima was puzzled, but she went on preparing supper.

Catherine received no word from Hassen and she phoned him. She was stunned when he said; "I'm sorry but I am unable to offer any help."

"But . . ."

"I regret it. I made a mistake. Please make some other arrangements. Goodbye."

With an effort of will, he banished Karim from his mind. Finding his composure again he enjoyed his evening meal, read the paper, and then retired to bed. Next morning he went to mosque as usual, but when he returned home he found Catherine there again. Angry that she should have come, he blurted out, "Listen to me, Catherine. I can't forgive him. For ten years he didn't care about me, whether I was alive or dead. Karim means nothing to me now."

"Why have you changed your mind? Do you find it so difficult to forgive him?"

"Don't talk to me of forgiveness. What forgiveness, when he threw me aside and chose to go with you? Let his white friends see to him, let Hillbrow see to him."

"Please, please, Mr. Hassen, I beg you . . ."

"No, don't come here with your begging. Please go away."

He opened the door and went out. Catherine burst into tears. Salima comforted her as best she could.

"Don't cry Caterine. All men hard. Dey don't understand."

"What shall I do now?" Catherine said in a defeated tone. She was an alien in the world of the non-whites. "Is there no one who can help me?"

"Yes, Mr. Mia help you," replied Salima.

In her eagerness to find some help, she hastily moved to the door. Salima followed her and from the porch of her home directed her to Mr. Mia's. He lived in a flat on the first floor of an old building. She knocked and waited in trepidation.

Mr. Mia opened the door, smiled affably, and asked her in.

"Come inside, lady; sit down . . . Fatima," he called to his daughter, "bring some tea."

Mr. Mia was a man in his fifties, his bronze complexion partly covered by a neatly trimmed beard. He was a well-known figure in the Indian community. Catherine told him of Karim and her abortive appeal to his brother. Mr. Mia asked one or two questions, pondered for a while, and then said, "Don't worry, my good woman. I'll speak to Hassen. I'll never allow a Muslim brother to be abandoned."

Catherine began to weep.

"Here, drink some tea and you'll feel better." He poured tea. Before Catherine left he promised that he would phone her that evening and told her to get in touch with him immediately should Karim's condition deteriorate.

Mr. Mia, in the company of the priest of the Newtown mosque, went to Hassen's house that evening. They found several relatives of Hassen's seated in the lounge (Salima had spread the word of Karim's illness). But Hassen refused to listen to their pleas that Karim should be brought to Newtown.

"Listen to me Hajji," Mr. Mia said. "Your brother can't be allowed to die among the Christians."

"For ten years he has been among them."

"That means nothing. He's still a Muslim."

The priest now gave his opinion. Although Karim had left the community, he was still a Muslim. He had never rejected the religion and espoused Christianity, and in the absence of any evidence to the contrary it had to be accepted that he was a Muslim brother.

"But for ten years he has lived in sin in Hillbrow."

"If he has lived in sin that is not for us to judge."

"Hajji, what sort of a man are you? Have you no feeling for your brother?" Mr. Mia asked.

"Don't talk to me about feeling. What feeling had he for me when he went to live among the whites, when he turned his back on me?"

"Hajji, can't you forgive him? You were recently in Mecca."

This hurt Hassen and he winced. Salima came to his rescue with refreshments for the guests.

The ritual of tea-drinking established a mood of conviviality and Karim was forgotten for a while. After tea they again tried to press Hassen into forgiving his brother, but he remained adamant. He could not now face Catherine without looking ridiculous. Besides he felt integrated now; he would resist anything that negated him.

Mr. Mia and the priest departed. They decided to raise the matter with the congregation in the mosque. But they failed to move Hassen. Actually his resistance grew in inverse ratio as more people came to learn of the dying Karim and Hassen's refusal to forgive him. By giving in he would be displaying mental dithering of the worst kind, as though he were a man without an inner fiber, decision, and firmness of will.

Mr. Mia next summoned a meeting of various religious dignitaries and received their mandate to transfer Karim to Newtown without his brother's consent. Karim's relatives would be asked to care for him, but if they refused, Mr. Mia would take charge.

The relatives, not wanting to offend Hassen and also feeling that Karim was not their responsibility, refused.

Mr. Mia phoned Catherine and informed her of what had been decided. She agreed that it was best for Karim to be amongst his people during his last days. So Karim was brought to Newtown in an ambulance hired from a private nursing home and housed in a little room in a quiet yard behind the mosque.

The arrival of Karim placed Hassen in a difficult situation and he bitterly regretted his decision not to accept him into his own home. He first heard of his brother's arrival during the morning prayers when the priest offered a special prayer for the recovery of the sick man. Hassen found himself in the curious position of being forced to pray for his brother. After prayers several people went to see the sick man; others went up to Mr. Mia to offer help. Hassen felt out of place and as soon as the opportunity presented itself he slipped out of the mosque.

In a mood of intense bitterness, scorn for himself, hatred of those who had decided to become his brother's keepers, infinite hatred for Karim, Hassen went home. Salima sensed her husband's mood and did not say a word to him.

In his room he debated with himself. In what way should he conduct himself so that his dignity remained intact? How was he to face the congregation, the people in the streets, his neighbors? Everyone would soon know of Karim and smile at him half sadly, half ironically, for having placed himself in such a ridiculous position. Should he now forgive the dying man and transfer him to his home? People would laugh at him, snigger at his cowardice, and Mr. Mia perhaps even deny him the privilege: Karim was now *his* responsibility. And what would Catherine think of him? Should he go away somewhere (on the pretext of a holiday) to Cape Town, to Durban? But no, there was the stigma of being called a renegade. And besides, Karim might take months to die; he might not die at all.

"O Karim, why did you have to do this to me?" he said, moving toward the window and drumming at the pane nervously. It galled him that a weak, dying man could bring such pain to him. An adversary could be faced, one could either vanquish him or be vanquished, with one's dignity unravished, but with Karim what could he do?

He paced his room. He looked at his watch; the time for afternoon prayers was approaching. Should he expose himself to the congregation? "O Karim! Karim!" he cried, holding on to the burglar-proof bar of his bedroom window. Was it for this that he had made the pilgrimage—to cleanse his soul in order to return into the penumbra of sin? If only Karim would die he would be relieved of his agony. But what if he lingered on? What if he recovered? Were not prayers being said for him? He went to the door and shouted in a raucous voice, "Salima!"

But Salima was not in the house. He shouted again and again, and his voice echoed hollowly in the rooms. He rushed into the lounge, into the kitchen; he flung the door open and looked into the yard.

He drew the curtains and lay on his bed in the dark.

Then he heard the patter of feet in the house. He jumped up and shouted for his wife. She came hurriedly.

"Salima, Salima, go to Karim, he is in a room in the mosque yard. See how he is, see if he is getting better. Quickly!"

Salima went out. But instead of going to the mosque, she entered her neighbor's house. She had already spent several hours sitting beside Karim. Mr. Mia had been there as well as Catherine—who had wept.

After a while she returned from her neighbor. When she opened the door her husband ran to her. "How is he? Is he very ill? Tell me quickly!"

"He is very ill. Why don't you go and see him?"

Suddenly, involuntarily, Hassen struck his wife in the face.

"Tell me, is he dead? Is he dead?" he screamed.

Salima cowered in fear. She had never seen her husband in this raging temper. What had taken possession of the man? She retired quickly to the kitchen. Hassen locked himself in the bedroom.

During the evening he heard voices. Salima came to tell him that several people, led by Mr. Mia, wanted to speak to him urgently. His first impulse was to tell them to leave immediately; he was not prepared to meet them. But he had been wrestling with himself for so many hours that he welcomed a moment when he could be in the company of others. He stepped boldly into the lounge.

"Hajji Hassen," Mr. Mia began, "please listen to us. Your brother has not long to live. The doctor has seen him. He may not outlive the night."

"I can do nothing about that," Hassen replied, in an audacious matter-of-fact tone that surprised him and shocked the group of people.

"That is in Allah's hand," said the merchant Gardee. "In our hands lie forgiveness and love. Come with us now and see him for the last time."

"I cannot see him."

"And what will it cost you?" asked the priest who wore a long black cloak that fell about his sandaled feet.

"It will cost me my dignity and my manhood."

"My dear Hajji, what dignity and what manhood? What can you lose by speaking a few kind words to him on his deathbed? He was only a young man when he left."

"I will do anything, but going to Karim is impossible."

"But Allah is pleased by forgiveness," said the merchant.

"I am sorry, but in my case the circumstances are different. I am indifferent to him and therefore there is no necessity for me to forgive him."

"Hajji," said Mr. Mia, "you are only indulging in glib talk and you know it. Karim is your responsibility, whatever his crime."

"Gentlemen, please leave me alone."

And they left. Hassen locked himself in his bedroom and began to pace the narrow space between bed, cupboard, and wall. Suddenly, uncontrollably, a surge of grief for his dying brother welled up within him.

"Brother! Brother!" he cried, kneeling on the carpet beside his bed and smothering his face in the quilt. His memory unfolded a time when Karim had been ill at the

Islamic Institute and he had cared for him and nursed him back to health. How much he had loved the handsome youth!

At about four in the morning he heard an urgent rapping. He left his room to open the front door.

"Brother Karim dead," said Mustapha, the Somali muezzin of the mosque, and he cupped his hands and said a prayer in Arabic. He wore a black cloak and a white skullcap. When he had done, he turned and walked away.

Hassen closed the door and went out into the street. For a moment his release into the street gave him a feeling of sinister jubilation, and he laughed hysterically as he turned the corner and stood next to Jamal's fruit shop. Then he walked on. He wanted to get away as far as he could from Mr. Mia and the priest who would be calling upon him to prepare for the funeral. That was no business of his. They had brought Karim to Newtown and they should see to him.

He went up Lovers' Walk and at the entrance of Orient House he saw the night watchman sitting beside a brazier. He hastened up to him, warmed his hands by the fire, but he did this more as a gesture of fraternization as it was not cold, and he said a few words facetiously. Then he walked on.

His morbid joy was ephemeral, for the problem of facing the congregation at the mosque began to trouble him. What opinion would they have of him when he returned? Would they not say he hated his brother so much that he forsook his prayers, but now that his brother is no longer alive he returns. What a man! What a Muslim!

When he reached Vinod's Photographic Studio he pressed his forehead against the neon-lit glass showcase and began to weep.

A car passed by filling the air with nauseous gas. He wiped his eyes, and looked for a moment at the photographs in the showcase; the relaxed, happy, anonymous faces stared at him, faces whose momentary expressions were trapped in film. Then he walked on. He passed a few shops and then reached Broadway Cinema where he stopped to look at the lurid posters. There were heroes, lusty, intrepid, blasting it out with guns; women in various stages of undress; horrid monsters from another planet plundering a city; Dracula.

Then he was among the quiet houses and an avenue of trees rustled softly. He stopped under a tree and leaned against the trunk. He envied the slumbering people in the houses around him, their freedom from the emotions that jarred him. He would not return home until the funeral of his brother was over.

When he reached the Main Reef Road the east was brightening up. The lights along the road seemed to be part of the general haze. The buildings on either side of him were beginning to thin and on his left he saw the ghostly mountains of mine sand. Dawn broke over the city and when he looked back he saw the silhouettes of tall buildings bruising the sky. Cars and trucks were now rushing past him.

He walked for several miles and then branched off onto a gravel road and continued for a mile. When he reached a clump of blue gum trees he sat down on a rock in the shade of the trees. From where he sat he could see a con-

stant stream of traffic flowing along the highway. He had
a stick in his hand which he had picked up along the road,
and with it he prodded a crevice in the rock. The action,
subtly, touched a chord in his memory and he was sitting
on a rock with Karim beside him. The rock was near a
river that flowed a mile away from the Islamic Institute.
It was a Sunday. He had a stick in his hand and he prodded at a crevice and the weather-worn rock flaked off and
Karim was gathering the flakes.

"Karim! Karim!" he cried, prostrating himself on the
rock, pushing his fingers into the hard roughness, unable
to bear the death of that beautiful youth.

He jumped off the rock and began to run. He would
return to Karim. A fervent longing to embrace his brother
came over him, to touch that dear form before the soil
claimed him. He ran until he was tired, then walked at
a rapid pace. His whole existence precipitated itself into
one motive, one desire, to embrace his brother in a final
act of love.

His heart beating wildly, his hair dishevelled, he
reached the highway and walked on as fast as he could.
He longed to ask for a lift from a passing motorist but
could not find the courage to look back and signal. Cars
flashed past him, trucks roared in pain.

When he reached the outskirts of Johannesburg it
was nearing ten o'clock. He hurried along, now and then
breaking into a run. Once he tripped over a cable and
fell. He tore his trousers in the fall and found his hands
were bleeding. But he was hardly conscious of himself,
wrapped up in his one purpose.

He reached Lovers' Walk, where cars growled around

him angrily; he passed Broadway Cinema, rushed toward Orient House, turned the corner at Jamal's fruit shop. And stopped.

The green hearse, with the crescent moon and stars emblem, passed by; then several cars with mourners followed, bearded men, men with white skullcaps on their heads, looking rigidly ahead, like a procession of puppets, indifferent to his fate. No one saw him.

Street Features

Zachariah Rapola

THE STREET COULD BE ANYWHERE. It stretches along an even gradient, punctuated by four-way junctions every five hundred meters or so. At longer intervals there are robots that maintain guard night and day. But, like any other mechanical thing, they become sick once in a while, so that instead of their electric winks and blinkings, the traffic is confronted by their human counterparts. But these too, like anything mortal, are prone to error—with the result that stretches of crawling motorcars idle and doze in that outstretched path. For in fact it is a path, like any in the bush, except that this one is decorated with tar, granite paving, and permanent yellow and white markings . . .

This is the street I dreamed about and longed for throughout my childhood. But now we are estranged. It has become possessed by four-wheeled chameleons, snails, sparrows, eagles, sharks, and whales, some of them

ZACHARIAH RAPOLA (1962–) is a filmmaker and the author of the collection of short stories *Beginnings of a Dream*, which won the 2008 NOMA award, and the youth novel *Stanza on the Edge*. He was awarded a fellowship to participate in the University of Iowa's International Writer's Program. He was born and raised in Alexandra, Johannesburg.

belching loudly and puffing smog from their narrow nostrils. Kites I longed to maneuver and chase after in its wide skies have been displaced, mocked by helicopters, gliders, airplanes, and all sorts of mechanical monsters that overwhelm and dwarf everything else up there.

This is a street I don't dream of anymore. It is now sandwiched between tall buildings, most of them not less than seven stories high. Often it slides a little way into squalor, but then municipality sanitation officers remember it. Kind-heartedly, they retrieve it from complete disintegration. This is usually on Saturday evenings or Sunday afternoons. Of course, it does get a nightly scrubbing, in the shape of garbage removal every evening around eight. Still, like a self-indulgent pig, it is back to its former state the following day, immediately after lunch time. I conclude that spring-cleaning for this street is hopeless.

My first observation, on seeing the street again after nearly ten years, was that it could be anywhere. It could be heaven, traveled by the few who've attained salvation. Or even hell, strewn with the multitudes of those who've flouted salvation—the revelry-drugged mob, swarming like ants around jam or bees over honey.

This view isn't mine alone, for those who see, use, and abuse the street every day, over and over again, are of the same verdict.

"But the path to heaven is narrow . . . doesn't the Bible testify to that?"

"Ya! That was before the clever ones died. The ones with an IQ of 150. They have probably introduced grinders and caterpillars there as well."

"That's sickening blasphemy."

"Don't you agree, heaven too needs to be modernized? Otherwise it would lose potential recruits to places like Sun City. Boy, flesh merchants have also awoken to the dangers of AIDS. They prescribe condoms. And that's modernization. I don't see any reason why heaven shouldn't go for a face-lift as well."

"Alley to social utopia!" bold newspaper headlines might shout.

"Red-light main road to moral degradation!" moralists might pronounce with condemnation.

Certainly the street is confused—just like all those who walk or drag themselves over its granite and tar. Going westward, one always has the unsettling feeling of approaching a lion's den, maybe because of the hot, smelly air that drifts from that direction. It is also like ascending an extremely steep hill. But going eastward is like fleeing a horde of living corpses with iron clamps chained to your ankles. It is a gentle down-slope, but the drag!

Some say it is a bewitched street. Others attribute its strangeness to perennial tremors caused by geological forces in its bowels. Still others say there is a natural pool underneath the street, where a great serpent lives. Its breathing is the cause of all the abnormal feelings people experience there.

The street also witnesses the birth of boys and girls. In adolescence they discover each other, drawn by the magnetic force that emanates from their loins. They become acquainted, become husbands and wives, and start copulating. Little children, some resembling them and others not resembling them, are born. Then age starts mistreating the children as they grow to adulthood. It is then that some choose to return to the rural areas, while others are hastily claimed by the grave.

It was here that the longing to meet a girl first took root in me. But because of my erratic stay, I was unable to stretch my roots deep enough for them to entangle and intertwine with those of a girl.

Were you to stop and inspect the street more appreciatively, you would see it differently. It is the kind of street that goes straight to wooing, grabbing, and clinging onto your affections. At one angle, it appears shaped like a maiden's torso. And men of all ages are in one way or another infatuated with that. There are times it appears like a Michelangelo sculpture, and women are ever consumed with trying to remodel their husbands' and boyfriends' age-battered and life-battered bodies on it.

At times I have seen young men, probably lonely ones, lie prostrate on its alabaster slabs. They weep silently, or roll around. Sometimes they behave obscenely, rocking themselves up and down. Embarrassed passers-by realize they are simulating love-making.

"Disgusting! Why don't they go buy it in Hillbrow."

Young women strolling with their boyfriends turn against them when walking on that street. Trouble starts when they first insist on taking off their shoes.

"He-wena! Ke eng tse, hee?"

"Let's lie down."

"Lie down! Where? Why?"

"Isn't it romantic? To let the wind caress you. To feel the pavement whisper and tickle your feet."

The boyfriends then either drag their girls away or slap them. But one or two try playing the game. And they pay the price. For, once down, the girls' attention is diverted—scribbling on the concrete what the boyfriends call nonsense, like "Sex me up" or "Shake-shake-shake,

shake your body," and similar song lyrics. After that they kiss the slab, whispering how gentle its touch is on their bodies, cooing how sweet it is. And the inference is quickly picked up by the boyfriends, even the dull ones:

"You mean I don't satisfy you, ne?"

Or, "Look here, Kedi! I don't dig your attitude."

"Huwii! Listen, he doesn't dig my attitude. What attitude is that, dear?"

"Kedi! Don't get funny, ne!" Whaaaa!—and a klap puts a stop to the women's funniness.

No! The street was never a piece of architectural genius. On closer inspection, especially with a microscope or magnifying glass, one notices little cracks here and there. There are bigger crevices in unsuspected places. These are places of refuge or asylum, where cents from the poor and rich alike are likely to wedge, therein to embrace posterity. They are spared the abuse of sweaty palms.

No! The street was never a piece of inspired technological engineering either. In many places, its edges have given in to the pressures of shoes and car tires. Careless drunkards now and then sprain ankles or even break fingers. A dozen naughty kids are always available to testify to the foul mood and erratic behavior of that street. Their bruised knees and foreheads and missing teeth are witness to that.

But the street has its patrons, lots and lots of them. The plain, the odd, the attractive, the rowdy, and ugly ones.

In the old days, Saturday afternoons meant "woza weekend." The inhabitants would creep out from their holes: laborers' top-floor rooms, ground-floor store-rooms . . . and on Sunday evenings they would disappear, to hole up again until the next weekend. At that point, when they chose to dematerialize, you would be unlikely to trace them. Even with the assistance of giant searchlights. For they had learned to evade the clutches of the Group Areas Act. It was at night that one could hear them whispering in muffled tones as they stole to deserted elevators, or indulged themselves in the pleasures of forbidden love.

Their life began after five, when the office workers and their bosses were gone. Then they would emerge, mothers with legions of children hanging on their aprons. Children whose fathers had forgotten their existence. Husbands with long-forgotten, rural wives; sons and daughters with bundu-confined parents. Again they would materialize. Appendages, human relics relegated to social scrap heaps. With the setting of the sun they would emerge: gangs of women reduced to selling their bodies for survival; vulturelike young men haunting bags, purses, and pockets; vagrants terrorizing dustbins and rubble piles for edibles.

After ten years, I came back, hoping to rekindle my acquaintance with the street. To end our estrangement and take up where we left off. Instead I met her . . .

Her name was Palesa, she told me. Her age was twenty-three. Her place of birth was Tsomo. In the Transkei, she added. I asked about her occupation. She looked me deep in the eyes, but would not tell. Her stare was bold, challenging, yet femininely sensuous. In the mirror-like center of her eyes, I saw childhood dreams gone wrong. Ambitions misdirected by ignorance and hopes betrayed by realities. I saw a whole existence derailed, immature ears crowded by a barrage of manipulative words—the snakes and ladders game of adolescence.

After a while she relaxed. She told me of the male cousins she stayed with. Then I noticed her bosom. It was limp, like a deflated balloon. It bore witness to an untimely motherhood. A motherhood that overnight had shuttled her from the harmonies of girlhood to the battering perils of single parenthood; that had served as a passport to exile. Away from the verbal abuse of parents, the scorn of neighbors and peers. From the jeers and sneers of former boyfriends. She had sought and found comfort in flight; whereupon the unknown had taken pity on her, welcomed and consoled her.

It was then that I realized everything she had told me about herself was not true—yet she was not a liar. She was a weaver of words. Words woven around her fragile inner being. Like Scheherazade, cheating loneliness and death by inventing stories of hope. Narrating them to herself. Constantly weaving courage, daring the possibilities of AIDS and other sexually transmitted diseases.

Two weeks later, I went to the corner on which we'd met. She was not there. I asked around for her. None of the girls seemed to know her. Her name was unfamiliar to most. I gave a short but desperate description, and then a few recalled her. I noted that in some of those recollections were evident both pleasure and spite, while in others I noticed pity.

"I last saw her with a white man in a red Sierra," one of the girls told me.

"No, no! It was a black man in a gray Golf," another insisted.

Did it matter or make any difference? Palesa, Melisa, or whoever she was, was nowhere. I noticed that some of the girls were eyeing me suspiciously, while others exhibited salespersons' interest, as if I might be persuaded into a deal. Finally, overcome by both uneasiness and pity, I turned away from them. Slowly I dragged myself westward. My eyes would now and then fasten on distant female figures and fish around their profiles for familiar features. At times my gaze would hook onto curb-crawling cars. Would she emerge from that car? Was it her, that one tucking her legs into the front seat?

My ears sucked onto familiar sounds: distant laughter, whistles, motorcar hooters. Would she emerge in a dazed rush for that one particular, favorite client? Would that car hooter or whistle nurse her from her sickbed or intensive care unit . . . or awaken her from the grave?

Where are you, dear one?

Would she tear free from the clutches of a new client for the customary caresses of her consistent client? Yet I knew I did not have the power or resources to rescue her. I couldn't re-dress the stage to offer her a better act. An act devoid of those beds, the posturing, the life-consuming embraces. Palesa or Melisa, or whoever she was, was no longer there. No more a feature of the street.

I fumbled along that merciless street. Now and then my vision would blur, and it was in such a state that she would become clearer . . . the one woman I might have loved. The one woman whose roots might have intertwined with mine to form a nourishing tree for little boys and girls of our own. That would have been possible, in another time and other circumstances.

In the end, she merged with the other insignificant particles of that street—artlessly laid granite paving stones, hurriedly leveled tar. Fresh and rain-stained cigarette stubs. Tastelessly graffitied walls and corners permeated with sulfuric urine odor. And here and there, orange and banana peels strewn around.

Cry, the Beloved Country
Alan Paton

THERE IS A LOVELY ROAD that runs from Ixopo into the hills. These hills are grass-covered and rolling, and they are lovely beyond any singing of it. The road climbs seven miles into them, to Carisbrooke; and from there, if there is no mist, you look down on one of the fairest valleys of Africa. About you there is grass and bracken and you may hear the forlorn crying of the titihoya, one of the birds of the veld. Below you is the valley of the Umzimkulu, on its journey from the Drakensberg to the sea; and beyond and behind the river, great hill after great hill; and beyond and behind them, the mountains of Ingeli and East Griqualand.

The grass is rich and matted, you cannot see the soil. It holds the rain and the mist, and they seep into the ground, feeding the streams in every kloof. It is well tended, and

---

ALAN PATON (1903–1988) is best known for his first novel *Cry, the Beloved Country,* of which this is the opening section, but he also authored biographies, short stories, poetry, and essays. He worked as a teacher for a decade before becoming the director of a reformatory for young offenders. With the advent of apartheid in 1948 Paton resigned that post and was a founding member and later president of the Liberal Party.

not too many cattle feed upon it; not too many fires burn it, laying bare the soil. Stand unshod upon it, for the ground is holy, being even as it came from the Creator. Keep it, guard it, care for it, for it keeps men, guards men, cares for men. Destroy it and man is destroyed.

Where you stand the grass is rich and matted, you cannot see the soil. But the rich green hills break down. They fall to the valley below, and falling, change their nature. For they grow red and bare; they cannot hold the rain and mist, and the streams are dry in the kloofs. Too many cattle feed upon the grass, and too many fires have burned it. Stand shod upon it, for it is coarse and sharp, and the stones cut under the feet. It is not kept, or guarded, or cared for, it no longer keeps men, guards men, cares for men. The titihoya does not cry here any more.

The great red hills stand desolate, and the earth has torn away like flesh. The lightning flashes over them, the clouds pour down upon them, the dead streams come to life, full of the red blood of the earth. Down in the valleys women scratch the soil that is left, and the maize hardly reaches the height of a man. They are valleys of old men and old women, of mothers and children. The men are away, the young men and the girls are away. The soil cannot keep them any more.

1949

Ronnie Govender

DUMISANE DID NOT SEE the chocolate wrappings. That was unusual for a scrupulously careful man. At three every morning, when he got up, he shut out everything else but his work which was probably why he was the last one to hear about the trouble in Tekweni. From the moment he got up from bed he was oblivious to everything but work. He was so caught up in his job as a bowser boy at the Model Garage that he didn't notice that there was an unusually big run on paraffin sales that day. It was his job to sell petrol—Simon sold the paraffin.

Everything had its place. He got up at three and made his tea. While the family slept, he blew alive the embers in the half-burnt logs in the stove. The ashes rose with the smoke and stung his nostrils, which received some relief from the pleasant aroma of boiling tea leaves. He would pour the steaming hot tea into his tin mug, always

RONNIE GOVENDER (1934–) was born in Cato Manor, outside Durban. His *At the Edge and Other Cato Manor Stories* received the Commonwealth Writers' Prize for the Africa region. Govender is also a playwright, and his works have been performed in countries around the world.

scorching his fingers in the process, and would step outside his two-roomed outhouse which he rented from Mr. Maniram.

He always paid his rent on time and Mr. Maniram liked him but kept his distance. Dumi felt slighted, but you couldn't easily find such good accommodation. The alternative was to live in Umkumbaan, the sprawling shanty town, where there was no water and no toilets. Yet you paid six pounds a month to Mr. Mohamed whose family also owned a shop on Booth Road. However, Mrs. Maniram, a kindly lady, had taken to his wife and every now and then would give the family some curry and bread.

While the family was still fast asleep, he walked from the bottom of Ashwell Road, past the smart brick house belonging to the garrulous bookkeeper, Mr. G. V. Naidoo, and which was grandly named "The Lion's Den." Mr. Naidoo was also an early riser. It was his practice to have his first smoke as he waited for his lift in front of his gate. Hau, this man could talk—even in Zulu!

"Woonjani, we Dumi?"

"Kona!"

"I see your shoes is shining special!"

But my shoes are always shining, thought Dumi. This man just felt he had to say something.

"Your teeth too!"

But my teeth are always shining too! Hau, this man should be an *imbongi*, a praise-singer, he is never short of words, but he is good for a laugh, and he would continue past Grammar Road, the short, steep road that led to the Cato Manor government-aided Indian School, built by the Indian community with the help of the Methodist Indian Mission. How nice if he could have sent his children there, but the government didn't allow that.

He walked past the Jew's shop which was where the white area started at the top of Cato Manor Road, the long road on the border which dissected the Indian area of Cato Manor from the area of the Berea. Onward to Concord Road which was a short, neat road flanked by staid brick-and-tile houses which could have been transplanted from some lower-middle-class English suburb. Their inhabitants in shorts, floppy hats, and sweaty red faces battled constantly to severely prune lush sub-tropica in a bid to transform it into lifeless gardens of well-ordered rows of hydrangea and meticulously manicured bougainvillea hedges. Dumi would contrast this soulless uniformity with the way nature celebrated the gift of life with such marvelous abandon on the banks of the Umgeni River, as it wound its way through the Valley of a Thousand Hills where he grew up as a child.

He would often long for the lush spontaneity of the Umgeni Valley, especially when he was chided by the mechanics for speaking loudly with his colleagues, "Can't you people keep your voices down? You're speaking to someone right next to you, not the other side of Booth Road, for chrissake!" In the valley there was lots of space and their voices rang out lustily, "Hau, unjani ukubeka, iphi wena hamba?" And after their conversations they would sing at the top of their voices.

There were times when he would forget where he was now and when he remembered, he would hasten to lower his voice in mid-sentence, "Hau, Mazibuko, what did you bring . . ." and he would drop his voice ". . . for lunch today?"

He had finished wiping a customer's car windscreen and was rushing to the next customer when he saw Mr. Osborne staring at the chocolate wrappings. Osborne didn't raise his voice, in fact, he didn't say anything. He just stood there, staring. Dumi was about to say that the noisy children in the Mercedes Benz had thrown the papers there, but decided not to. Mr. Osborne's fixed glare told him, "It's your job. I'm paying you for it. I want my garage to be spotless, no matter how busy you are."

No histrionics. You either did exactly what he wanted or you collected your final pay packet on Friday, but if you worked hard you were adequately rewarded. He didn't fire his staff and he never called you "kaffir" either. He passed on his family's old clothes to his staff. In fact, the clothes weren't all that old—they looked posh on his wife when she wore them to church on Sunday. Percival Osborne himself worked hard. His father, the son of a British settler, worked long hours and eventually became a wealthy wholesale merchant with a thriving import-export business and shares in two of the biggest multinationals in the country. He had taken care not to pamper his children and Percival inherited the old man's ability for hard work, and his sense of independence. He wasn't as spectacularly successful as his father, but he wasn't exactly poor. Dumi recalled the splendor of the Osborne family mansion on their sprawling Kloof estate when he drove the *Baas* and his family there to a New Year's Eve party. On certain occasions, when the Baas was going to have drinks, Dumi acted as chauffeur. He had seldom seen such splendid suits and dresses, such dazzling jewelry. There was even a live band. The neighbors were invited, so they didn't mind the noise. In any event, the nearest house was about a quarter of a mile down the road, separated by huge trees and parkland.

What a party it was!

Well into the evening, when everyone had had a few drinks, some put their arms around Dumi and his colleagues, offering them drinks and snacks, even the women!

"Come on, have a drink, Dumi!"

"Thanks, Baas."

"What will you have?"

"I'll have beer, Baas; just one."

"Beer? On a night like this? Don't be silly, have some brandy."

"I'm driving, Baas."

"Don't worry, I won't tell your Baas."

And the glass was thrust into his hands. Osborne didn't notice because by then he himself had had enough drinks. They even asked Dumi to sing. He sang regularly in the church choir. He shyly declined at first, but after a couple of drinks he was in the mood. He secretly hoped that the offers would persist.

"No, Baas, I'm not a very good singer."

"Come on Dumi, all blacks can sing."

"Yes, can't they? They have such marvelous voices."

"Now please, not one of those churchy numbers, for chrissake!"

"But negro spirituals are such jazzy stuff, darling."

"Oh, when the saints
Go marching in
Oh, when the saints
Go marching in . . .

Burp! Oh, I beg your pardon."
"You'd be better off singing . . .

Whisky rye whisky
Whisky I cry
If whisky don't kill me
I'll live till I die . . . burp!"

Dumi thought, *Hau, why doesn't he shut up and let me sing?*

"Hey, come on, it's Dumi's turn—ladies and gentlemen, I give you Satchmo Dumi Armstrong, hau!"

"No, not Satchmo, you idiot, Dumi sings like Mario Lanza."

After a few bars of Mario Lanza's "Because," there was a hush in the revelry. They listened in growing admiration and awe. At the end there was a burst of enthusiastic applause and they thrust ten pound notes into his hands.

"Amazing! Where did you learn to sing like that? Can you imagine a bowser boy singing like that? Can you?"

"Pity, if he were white he would have been singing at a beachfront hotel or on the radio."

"For chrissake, don't get away; you know what will happen to the toilets, my deah!"

"Where did you learn to sing like that?"

"I listen to the radio while I'm working and I listen and I learn."

"Simply marvelous."

"I told you it comes to them naturally, my deah."

The music, the laughter, the dancing and the fun! Someone pushed him into the pool. He almost drowned.

"Hau, I can't swim, I can't swim!"

Henry, the boss's jovial friend who had a rosy complexion for most of the day, jumped in fully clothed to save him. Others jumped in too and the party was in full swing. As the clock struck twelve everybody started singing, "Auld Lang Syne" and "Happy New Year," including those in the water. Dumi, shivering, singing, and hanging on to the side of the pool, marveled at such happiness and togetherness. Everybody's so happy. Why only on New Year's Eve? Why not every day?

∼

Osborne expected everyone to work as hard as he did. He seldom shouted or said an angry word, but he wasn't friendly either. Indeed, he believed that people should be kept in their places. The races were different and that's the way they should stay. He was quite happy as long as that rule was not broken. In fact, he could be quite nice, but heaven help those who broke the rule. The only time Dumi saw him completely lose his temper, his face blazing red, nostrils flaring, and tiny beads of sweat on his forehead and pock-marked nose, was when the Mahomedy family had moved into the double-story house opposite the garage on the corner of Gillits and Jan Smuts Roads. It was quite an event.

Everyone at the garage stood watching as the newcomers, with the women in their hijaars, moved into the house. It was the year 1949 and by then the Durban Municipality had passed the notorious Pegging Act, the forerunner of the Group Areas Act. The legislation was intended to "peg the encroaching hordes of Indians and Blacks to their boundaries." However, a blind eye was turned to the encroachment of a few wealthy Indians. The Mahomedys were unlike the other Indians who were Dumi's neighbors in Cato Manor. These people were as fair-skinned as the whites and were rich and well-dressed. Their furniture was expensive and they had two brand-new cars. Dumi's neighbors in Cato Manor, with the exception of a few like Moodley who owned buses, and Persadh who owned a small furniture factory, were not wealthy people. If they were not market gardeners, they were either laborers like himself, or they worked in factories.

Looking at the Mahomedys move in, right next to the garage, Osborne was livid, "Why in God's name, don't these people go and live with the rest in their own areas? Why do they insist on living with us?"

And it was the only time Dumi heard him swearing, "Bloody bastards! Give them an inch and they take a yard. They should send them all back to India. They breed like damn flies!"

Dumi had picked up the chocolate wrappings and was taking them back to the bin that stood next to the workshop when he saw the Baas in animated conversation with the mechanic, Sullivan, and his two African grease-monkeys. This was unusual because although Sullivan was white, the Baas actually kept his distance from him.

Sullivan, who smoked and swore a lot, called him *Sir*. He caught snatches of the conversation, ". . . they should terrorize the pigs until they go back to India," ". . . paraffin will do the job," and ". . . they deserve it."

He was much too busy to stand and listen although his curiosity was roused by such unusual talk. It made sense later when he saw his friend Poobal, who also worked as a petrol attendant on Bellair Road for the Seebrans. Poobal was in a car packed with solemn people. He looked very agitated, "Sawubona, Poobal; unjani?"

Poobal nodded in greeting. Funny, he was always talkative. He spoke Zulu fluently and they were always poking fun at each other, "In indaba, Poobal?"

Poobal told him that there was a lot of fighting in the Indian Market on Victoria Street. An Indian stallholder had caught an African boy stealing and had punished him. Africans attacked the stallholder and were soon attacking all Indians in their way.

"They were fighting in town, we got nothing to do with that."

"So why are you frightened?"

"Some white people are stirring up the trouble. Trucks from the big firms are taking some tsotsis to Cato Manor, Riverside and all the other places where Indians live and are giving them petrol and paraffin. Some firms are closing early so that their workers can attack us. We can't fight them. We are too few."

"But why never call the police?"

"The police know. They are just standing and watching. We are taking the families to Maritzburg to my cousin's house. We'll be safe there."

That explained why so many Africans were coming to the garage. The garage also sold paraffin in bottles, but the sales had never been so good. Osborne was chatting to some of the staff in Zulu. Dumi could hardly believe his ears. He was joking with them about burning down the houses of the Indians. Perhaps he didn't realize these people were serious. Reports were coming in of houses and shops being looted and burnt and of people being assaulted, raped, and killed. Dumi was aghast. Perhaps the stories were being exaggerated.

At about half past three, Osborne called his staff together. Dumi listened in stunned silence, "The Indians deserve what they are getting. They make a lot of money from you people and they have no respect for you."

Some of the workers agreed volubly.

"This is your country. We white people have come to improve it for you. We have built roads, hospitals, schools, and shops. These people have only come to make money. They have houses. You haven't. You can tell your friends they can have all the paraffin they want, free of charge!"

When Osborne had gone back to his office, Dumi pleaded with his friends in hushed tones, "We are Christians. These people are our friends. Only a few are rich. The rest are poor, like us. This is wrong."

He told them about Poobal who did the same job as he was doing. Together with his brothers who worked in factories, they built a brick house and were sending all their children to school. Poobal's son was studying to become a teacher. He told them about R. D. Naidu and Billy Peters who were fighting against the color bar and who were being thrown into jail all the time for their beliefs. Simon and Johannes, who were about his age, agreed with him but the others told him bluntly that the Baas was right. That evening the arson, looting, and raping increased. The smell of petrol and paraffin were in the air and the night sky was lit up by soaring flames.

It was a matter of time before the rampaging mob got to Ashwell Road. Indian families with cars were fleeing. The Manirams didn't have a car and Dumi found them huddled together in their bedroom. It was the first time he had ever entered the house. The youngest child screamed when he saw Dumi. Mrs. Maniram was sobbing quietly, "My children, my children!"

"Numzaan, it is not wise to stay here. They will come any time now."

Mr. Maniram was a brave man, but all he had was a huge kitchen knife.

"We have nowhere to go. They will have to kill me before they can touch my family."

"You are alone, you cannot fight so many. You must hide in my house. That's the only way."

Mr. Maniram hesitated. Mrs. Maniram sprang into action. She bundled the children into the outhouse and the family were hidden under the beds and in the wardrobes. The mob had worked its way up Ashwell Road and they could hear the sounds of the war chants above the screams of terrified people. Dumi and his wife stood outside as the mob appeared.

"What are you doing here? This is amaKula's house."

"I stay here. I am renting this house."

"Where are the people from the main house?"

"They've run away."

"You're lying."

Some ran into the main house and after ransacking it, set fire to it. The flames lit the entire area.

"They're not in the house. They must be in your house!"

"Listen, my brother. I don't like the amaKulas myself. Please don't go in and frighten my children."

The crowd stood around hesitantly. Suddenly a young man broke from the crowd and dashed into the house. Within seconds he was out shouting, "He's lying. They're hiding under the beds!"

All mercy deserted them.

It deserted the souls of fathers, mothers, sons, and daughters, giving way to the savagery that lurks eternally in the human heart. Out of the time warp of primeval hate flew the spear. It shot through Dumi's chest. There was no pity, no reason in the hearts of these malleable souls, held captive by minds more savage in their cunning—the cunning on which empires have been built.

Mating Birds

Lewis Nkosi

IN A FEW DAYS I AM TO DIE. Strange, the idea neither shocks nor frightens me. What I feel most frequently
now is a kind of numbness, a total lack of involvement in
my own fate, as though I were an observer watching the
last days in the life of another man.

Every morning I stand at this small grilled window,
gazing at the sky, which is a marvelous blue at this time of
year; the air is as clear, as hard as frost, and the sunlight
has a soft shimmering quality to it: it blinds the eye; it
dazzles. Sometimes a flock of birds will ascend the sky,
wings beating wildly; often a pair will mate up there in
freedom and open space, clinging to each other joyfully
in the bright air as though for dear life. Then, no longer
able to restrain himself, the male will attempt to inject
his sperm into the female and he, of course, as often as
not, will miss so that you can see his pale seed dripping

LEWIS NKOSI (1938–), a journalist in South Africa, left the
country in 1961 when he received a scholarship to study at Har-
vard. He has subsequently taught at universities in the United
States, Zambia, and Poland and published novels, essays, and
plays. This piece is from his novel *Mating Birds*.

through the air while the female giggles wildly, as is the habit of her sex.

The scenario is the same every morning. The mating birds caw, they whir and whirl outside my window and the smell of fresh spring sharpens the air with its lush, acrid promise. All the same, it is mostly the birds pairing in the open sky that remind me with a vivid poignancy I rarely feel these days why I'm locked up in this tiny cell, awaiting death by execution. I move my hand toward the window and the sunlight, and try to imagine the colors of the Indian Ocean in the early morning light when the water is already flecked with brilliant sunspots or in the early afternoon when, hardly moving at all, the water turns into shiny turquoise.

I can see it all quite clearly: the beach, the children's playgrounds, the seafront hotels, and the sweating, pink-faced tourists from up-country; the best time of all is that silent, torpid hour of noon when the beach suddenly becomes deserted and, driven back to the seafront res-taurants and the temporary shelter of their hotel rooms, crowds of sea bathers suddenly vanish, leaving behind them not only the half-demolished cheese and tomato sandwiches but sometimes an occasional wristwatch, an expensive ring, or a finely embroidered handkerchief still smudged with lipstick from a pair of anonymous lips. Not infrequently, the tourists leave behind them an even wor-thier trophy—a young body lying spent and motionless on the warm white sands to be gazed at by us, the silent forbidden crowds of non-white boys in a black, mutinous rage.

That, after all, is how I first saw the English girl one

afternoon, lying on an empty stretch of Durban beach as though washed up by the tide after an all-night storm: she was a golden statue, lovely and broken among the ruins of an ancient city, and yet for all that, she was shockingly alive, dripping suntan oil and glowing with the sun that beat upon her elongated body. Her flesh was surrendered, as it were, to the hungry gaze of African youths who combed the beach every day for lost or discarded articles.

Maiden Outing to Rondebosch

Jan Rabie

THE DAY AFTER the *Vogelsang* dropped anchor in the bay the commander gave all the Netherlands women an opportunity of traveling to the *ronde bos* [circular patch of bush]. Never before had any of them gone farther than a mile or two into the interior of the strange, perilous land, but all were only too eager for a chance of getting away from the fort.

At crack of dawn the five matrons and the three young girls, whispering and giggling, settled themselves on the wagon. Amid the laughter and cheers of the escorting soldiers and infantrymen the commander dashingly swung himself onto his horse and raised his hand as a signal. A gun-salute boomed from the walls of the fort, the echo rebounded from the Table Mountain, and the sound died away over the bay which was lightly brushed by a gentle breeze from the west. At once the drivers shouted to their oxen, and the creaking wheels began to turn.

The clumsy wagon of Cape wood and the rugged

JAN RABIE (1920–2001) was one of the twentieth century's foremost Afrikaans authors. A prolific novelist, short story writer, essayist, and travel writer, he was awarded France's *Légion d'honneur.*

road had the women frequently clutching at each other or hastily disposing their dresses. The stately Mevrou de Stael, especially, seated up in front beside her sister-in-law Maria van Riebeeck, was hard put to hold firmly onto the luncheon basket and maintain her dignity. Yet it was a real pleasure excursion. The sallies of Antjie die Boerin who was holding her latest scion of many, the six-week-old Dirkie in one practiced arm while indicating the scenery with the other; the excited exclamations of the girls, Cornelia Boom and Christina and Petronella Does; the fresh summer morning smelling of aromatic herbs; the unfamiliar cornet-shaped flowers as large as saucers growing on the slopes of the Windberg; and perhaps, too, a subconscious awareness of the significance of the outing, had made each woman there experience a glad tingling as never before in all their four and a half years at the Cape, the hard, hungry years of struggling to get a foothold on the southern tip of Africa.

More than the others Maria sensed that this was an exceptional day. After so many nights of lying awake and hearkening she knew all about her husband's cherished plan: that now, after the blessing and providence of God, the Dutch settlement should be established even more securely with the aid of free-burghers—the first colonists.

A smile lit up and softened her face every time she noted how her husband would spur impatiently ahead and then ride back again at a gallop to point out something they ought certainly not to miss. His slight, vibrant figure, impeccable in fine broadcloth set off with silver cord above the rich garters and stockings of Napolese silk, reassured her and confirmed her thoughts: he has a right to be proud of what he has achieved so far, and to feel optimistic about what lies ahead.

Beside her Mevrou de Stael spoke, "If only Jan does not need to spoil his fine clothes again by having to embrace the greasy, sooty Hottentots!"

"Yet I should like to see the commander cutting capers with them," Antjie quipped irreverently.

Mevrou de Stael's disapproving eye quickly changed the girls' suppressed laughter into hasty speculations about other possible dangers. Such as lions, for instance, or the hyena that was shot as recently as the Saturday before last. With stealthy glances and delicious tremors they observed the armed soldiers before and behind the wagon, and then asked whether they might get down and walk a bit. But their mothers refused curtly, and made them pull their skirts down even more decorously.

For the troops and foot soldiers, mostly young and unmarried, it was also an out-of-the-ordinary day. One of them, Elbert Dirksen, had such goggling calf's eyes for the elder of the two Does maidens, the sixteen-year-old Christina, that his mates began to chaff him, till the corporal sent him ahead to roll rocks out of the road.

Whenever they paused to give the beasts a breather and allow the men a draw at their pipes, Christina was blushing with crimson cheeks. The worst part was the teasing of the mischievous Cornelia who was no older than she and would be marrying the second gardener in four months' time. Even the commander's wife had to lean over and, under the pretext of settling Petronella's headband, chide the girls, yet softly so that the menfolk shouldn't hear.

Noon was still far off when they came to the new lands close to the *ronde bos*. Here the soil was richer and the mountain even more beautiful, romantic and crenellated like a castle wall with deep, craggy battlements. At the little guardhouse everyone got off.

The commander immediately led the ladies off to view the wheat and tobacco fields within a sturdy paling. He drew attention to everything: the clover field where three men were making hay, the young apple and orange trees, the luxuriant Turkish and Roman beans, the full heavy ears of wheat which the harsh south-easter could never blast here in the shelter of the mountain.

"And all this has been accomplished in only six months. Just imagine what a number of industrious farmers could produce here," he exclaimed enthusiastically and gestured with his Gouda pipe, that had long since gone out, to embrace the whole valley of the Liesbeek River.

"The honorable Company could really not do better than lay out permanent farms here."

Beside him his wife nodded approvingly, but half distracted like the other women, enchanted by the splendor of the bushy landscape and the luxuriant golden corn below the mountain's flanks.

"Indeed, it is more beautiful even than in the fatherland," one of them sighed dreamily—Janneke Boddys who had arrived at the Cape only recently.

"For the young children this is already their fatherland," someone else said.

"Well now, I don't know," Janneke objected, "what about all the savage natives that . . ." But her words were swallowed by the commander's laugh. The roguish and daring Cornelia had come from behind and placed her hands over his eyes as he was trying to relight his pipe, and in a high falsetto voice she now demanded that he should guess who it was otherwise he would remain "blind-man's-buff." The commander good-naturedly entered into the spirit of the prank.

Wherever they went the corporal and his six men followed at a short distance. Herry [leader Khoi/Hottentot band] and his treacherous minions were still skulking around here somewhere, near the Bush Hill, though, in truth, shivering with fear like a lady's lapdog whenever he saw a Dutchman; but a guilt-ridden Hottentot is also a dangerous one. When the girls kept straying off carelessly the corporal respectfully asked them please to keep close to the party.

It was Maria who finally persuaded her husband to return to the thatched watch-post, where Antjie Boom was expertly arranging the picnic luncheon. The two sentries had betimes gathered green branches and erected a cool shady bower against one of the turf-built walls. While the commander in his restless way was still supervising elsewhere and giving instructions, the women spread cloths, laid out the cutlery, and seated themselves serenely in the shade. Antjie die Boerin detracted somewhat from the genteel scene, by loosening her clothing and beginning to suckle her baby. Mevrou de Stael found it expedient to direct the sentries' attention to their duty of standing somewhat farther off to watch out for advancing hordes of Hottentots.

The portly Antjie looked after the men and sighed, "The poor things, they do not see a baby every day."

The women were so convulsed with laughter that quite a few dress fastenings had to be unobtrusively slackened.

The commander arrived at last and smiling at his wife he asked, "Well, well, and are the ladies enjoying the day out?" Satisfied with the reply, he turned to the soldier who had come to stand ramrod stiff as a sentinel near him. "No, no, Dirksen," he said, "go and relax: for you and the others today is also a holiday."

"All men are as blind as moles," the daughter of Janneke Boddys whispered to Christina, and was given a little pinch in reply.

Everything went merrily, except for a troublesome wasp that made Janneke sit rigid with tightly closed eyes while she asked repeatedly in a trembling voice, "Is it still there?"

After the repast the commander led them higher up to see the mountain stream and the work of woodcutting in the forest.

It was hot: still, balmy warmth like the feel of a sleeper's skin. The young women were constantly running ahead, but the older women were slower, quieter, and more sedate, as if the sight of the men's activity all around to tame the new rich earth made them realize more acutely that they were women and mothers of children.

The mountain stream whispered its soft urgency through the languid summer afternoon, and in the bush the doves cooed and the echoes of the axe strokes resounded from the nearby crags. Once some foresters passed close to them with two ponderous, straining oxen hauling a balk of timber for the pier. Later on and higher up they were able to overlook the glorious landscape, far

out to beyond the neck between Bush Hill and the mountain, where they could just descry tiny cattle grazing near
the little brown hive-like huts of the Cape-men.

Jan van Riebeeck explained everything: where a mill to
grind the wheat could be erected beside the stream, and
which of the sturdy yellowwood trees they would try to
preserve. His wife listened as attentively as possible but
the faint smile hovering about her lips wavered at times
to betray some trepidation, especially when the growth of
trees began to draw in more densely and the close, dank
odor of moss enfolded them.

"We've come far enough now, Jan," she warned gently.
"See, the others are getting tired."

But now a search had to be made for two of the girls
who had strayed farther ahead, accompanied by one of
the soldiers. The commander sent two others to call them
back, and the women sat down to rest. Only poor Mevrou de Stael remained standing in order to conceal a torn
stocking beneath the stately tent of her dress.

A flower had been the cause of this interruption. The
soldier, Elbert Dirksen, had told the girls about a waxen
red flower growing just off the narrow track, and of course
they had to go and examine it. Awkward and trembling
he had plucked one for Christina and she scolded him for
his vandalism. And then her younger sister had to run to a
great yellowwood tree, after borrowing his knife, to carve
out her name.

"This will remain here very, very long," she said, pout-
ing prettily, and proceeded to add the date: 5 December
1656.

Suddenly Christina gave a little scream. Framed in the

wild foliage were two brown faces staring open-mouthed at her.

Elbert immediately reached for his flintlock, but the Hottentots laid down their bundles of spears and with expressions of crafty pleading made signs with their hands.

When the girls backed away, the Hottentots emerged from the shrubbery, their mantles of oxhide draped proudly over their shoulders, and their necks and wrists glistening with copper circlets. They did not look at the soldier, only at the young girl. Then there was a thrashing in the bush where the blue tunics of more soldiers appeared, and suddenly one of the Hottentots began to stammer in broken Hollands, "Why you drive us away?" And in hesitant, apprehensive pride he called again to the girls, "Why you want to take our land?"

Then the two soldiers came up with leveled muskets, and he and his companion sprang round and vanished into the bush.

"Wh . . . what . . . why did he. . . talk so to me?" the girl stuttered.

"They often plague us like this, ever since we began the fields and the watch-posts here, but we only wish to raise food for ourselves . . ." Elbert began to explain.

But his fellow soldiers laughed, "Oh, forget the savage heathens. Eh, Christina, you lovely thing?" And boldly they wanted to touch her and Petronella. Giggling and coy, the two sisters warded off their eager hands and ran back to the little path where the others were waiting.

A little while later, after the girls had been thoroughly reprimanded by their mother, and the commander had praised the soldiers for not acting over-hastily, the stroll back to the guardhouse was resumed. No afternoon could possibly be more beautiful, and more soothingly evoke obliviousness to care.

When the shadow of the mountain began to lengthen Maria became restless to return to the fort where her youngest had been left in the sole care of a young slave girl. Antjie's sleeping infant, who had been carried a while by an embarrassed soldier, now also awoke protesting loudly.

Tired yet satisfied, they all gathered by the wagon. But before they left, the commander celebrated the memorable day by distributing tobacco and broaching a small vat of Spanish wine. Those of the ladies who wished were given some, as also the male escort, who jubilantly proposed a rousing toast to this maiden journey of the ladies, the founders of the nation.

Finally the commander clapped his hands for silence and called, "We're leaving now. Think well whether we've forgotten anything!"

Nobody had; only Christina looked perplexed for a moment as if she were trying to think.

Then a box was placed beside the wagon to enable the older women to ascend. The soldiers fell in again, and the procession started off light-heartedly from the *ronde bos*, back to the fort in Table Bay. In front rode Jan van Riebeeck, dapper and elegant as always on his horse that tomorrow would be drawing heavy loads again.

The trumpeter was among the infantry, and Antjie Boom asked him please to blow the rust from his throat. Which he proceeded to do with good heart. In this changed, contented, yet somewhat subdued mood, they fell to singing, one by one. Past the golden-crowned corn field and for long stretches of the peaceful road homeward the men and women sang gay songs and sad ones, also the one they all remembered best: the national anthem, the "Wilhelmus van Nassauwe."

Translated from the Afrikaans by Wally Smuts

Morning 1955

Richard Rive

I REMEMBER

those who used to live in District Six, those who lived
on Caledon Street and Clifton Hill and busy Hanover
Street. There are those of us who still remember the ripe,
warm days. Some of us still romanticize and regret when
our eyes travel beyond the dead bricks and split tree-
stumps and wind-tossed sand.

When I was a boy and chirruping ten, a decade after
the end of the Second World War, when I was Tarzan
and Batman and could sing "Rainbow on the River"
like Bobby Breen—in those red-white-and-blue days I
remember especially the weekends, which began with the
bustle of Friday evenings when the women came home
early from the factories and the men came home late

RICHARD RIVE (1931–1989) was a teacher, literary critic,
novelist, and author of short stories. Hailing from District Six,
the multiracial area adjacent to Cape Town's central business
district that was declared a white area in 1966 and razed almost
entirely, he is known for his wry humor and wit. Rive's work
has been translated into many languages. This is an excerpt
from his novel *"Buckingham Palace," District Six.*

---

although they had been paid off early—and the feeling of well-being and plenty in our house on the upper left-hand side of Caledon Street near St. Mark's Church. We lived in the fourth in a row of five moldy cottages called "Buckingham Palace" by the locals. The first, 201, the one farthest from the church as if by design, was a bluepainted House of Pleasure called the "Casbah." In it lived Mary and The Girls. Next to them at 203, painted bright pink, was "Winsor Park" (spelt like that), which was occupied by Zoot and The Boys. Then came 205, the cottage of The Jungles, then ours, then at 209 that of Last-Knight the barber, his wife, and three daughters. A sprawling open field overgrown with weeds and rusty tin cans separated Buckingham Palace from the church.

Friday evenings were warm and relaxed.

We felt mellow because it was the weekend and payday. While my sister got dressed to go to the Star or National Bioscope with her boyfriend, since there was no time for her to cook I was sent to Millard's Fish and Chips shop beyond Tennant Street to get the evening's supper. I raced with the south-easter and then forced my way into the shop crowded with customers, the air thick with the smell of stale sawdust, boiling fish oil, and sweaty bodies as steam rose from the frying pans. When I had wriggled my way through the forest of grown-up legs and torsos, I found myself jammed against the counter, always just too late to order from the last batch of fish and chips, and then had to wait, fighting to prevent the breath from being squeezed out of my body, until the next batch of gleaming stockfish and thick fingers of potato chips were hoisted, dripping oil, and spewed out onto the warmers. On the way home I raced to keep the parcels hot, but not so fast that I could not pierce a small hole in the packet and remove a few chips. But this was finally detected by my hawk-eyed mother, who knew what was happening in spite of my denials.

Saturdays and Sundays were different.

Saturday mornings were brisk, for some men must work and all women must shop. And Hanover Street was crowded and the bazaars and fish market did a roaring trade. There were groceries to buy on the book and clothes on hire-purchase.

Katzen, who was the landlord of Buckingham Palace, had his emporium on the corner of Hanover and Tennant Streets. His shop windows were cluttered with bric-à-brac such as celluloid dolls, huge glass tankards still celebrating the Coronation, rolls of crêpe de chine, gramophones and framed and mounted prints of a violently pink-faced King George VI and Queen Elizabeth. After his premises had been broken into six times in so many weeks, Katzen displayed a notice outside his shop, "Although Katzen has been burgled again, Katzen will never burgle you!" We all knew that there was no chance of the small, Jewish shopkeeper with his walrus mustache and large feet ever climbing through our back windows to steal our radios, but we also felt that he could rob us in other ways. The thieves always seemed to steal his gramophones and crêpe de chine and patriotically left the prints of King George VI and his queen.

Saturday mornings Tennant Street, Hanover Street, and Castle Bridge heaved and bustled with housewives, peddlers, skollies, urchins, pimps and everybody else. Everybody bought everything on lay-bye and it was all written down in exercise books; Moodley, the Indian general dealer on Caledon Street, scribbled it on the back of brown paper bags which he lost when he absent-mindedly used them as containers for sugarbeans or rice. Everyone also knew they would have to pay in the end, even those who owed Moodley, although when that end was, was extremely flexible and it could be next week or next year or next never.

Near Seven Steps Mr. Angelo Baptiste owned a dark Italian shop from the ceiling of which hung strings of garlic. His shop also smelt of macaroni and olive oil. We would tease him in order to hear him swearing volubly in his native language.

On Saturday afternoons I went to Star Bioscope with Estelle, Manne, and Broertjie to see that week's exciting episode of "Zorro Rides Again" in black and white. We could not stand in any queue to get in because the idea of queues had not yet reached District Six. So we pushed and tugged and sweated to slip through the narrow opening in the iron gates which would allow us into the foyer where we could purchase tickets. Estelle, who never feared anyone, simply climbed onto the nearest pair of shoulders at the back of the heaving mass and then crawled over heads. Once through the gates, we bought our tickets to sit on the hard seats downstairs, where ushers in soiled, prison-warden khaki, shouted loudly and forced us to share seats with whomever they shoved down beside us. If you raised any objections you were meanly clouted. (One sadistic usher took to riding up and down the aisle on a bicycle, lashing out with his belt at any unfortunate urchin who provoked his displeasure.) When Estelle, resplendent in his cowboy shirt, three-quarter pants, and

high-heeled boots, arrived late and stood in the lighted
entrance, he would cup his hands to his mouth and blow
a loud strident whistle which only he could blow. It rose
above the packed and heaving auditorium to Manne, who
sat in the farthermost corner tight between his girl and
the one he was keeping for Estelle. Manne, heeding the
whistle of his leader, would throw lighted matches into
the air, regardless of anyone on whom it landed, like a
ship sending up distress flares. And then Estelle would
wade over seats and frightened urchins in a straight line
to his minion and the girl reserved for him.

We sat goggle-eyed in the thick, cigarette-smoke dark,
watching Zorro carve out Z's with his whip on the foreheads of those crooks stupid enough to challenge his dex-
terity with inferior weapons like six-guns. We munched
our way through half-loaves of split-open brown bread
that had whole pieces of fried fish placed in between.
Estelle, who was a successful pickpocket, always paid for
the refreshments. When they played the movie of Ham-
let, Estelle whistled and shouted derisively that it was a
lot of balls, and Alfie, who was in Junior Certificate at
Trafalgar High and a budding critic, said the outjie spoke
far too much and who ever saw a ghost that looked like
that.

And in the evenings we would stand in hushed door-
ways and tell stories about the legendary figures of District Six, Zoot, Pretty-Boy and Mary, or show off about
our prowess with the local girls, or just talk about the
ways of white folks and how Cissie Gool was fighting for
us and showing the white people a thing or two. And how
wonderful it was to live in America and talk like Charles

Starrett and sing like Gene Autry. The young men went to parties or bioscope, and the older men played dominoes and klawerjas on the stoeps, holding the huge boards between them on their laps; and when they banged down the dominoes or the cards, hordes of flies would spin up and then settle down again. The young girls waited for the men to fetch them, all coy, demure, and made up in the latest fashions. The older housewives came out with their wooden benches and sat apart from the men on the stoep and gossiped the mild evening away.

And the apricot warmth of a summer Sunday morning when almost everyone slept late and moldy cocks kept in postage-stamp, asphalt yards crowed their confined calls to wake no one in particular. Then the sun rose over-ripe although it was barely six o'clock and the whole District was snoring and blowing away the fumes of Saturday evening. The gaiety and sheer abandonment of the previous night had given way to the exhausted sleep of Sunday morning.

I would be sent to buy koeksisters for breakfast at a house next to Bernstein's Bottle Store, where three unmarried Muslim sisters lived. Their house always smelt of aniseed and rose water. I would stand in the dark passage awaiting my turn, watching them fry the light dough until it was golden brown, then dip it hot and sugary into coconut. They had taken a liking to me and always gave me an extra one wrapped separately which I ate on the way back.

When the first people had woken from their smoke-filled sleep, the more righteous washed themselves in zinc tubs in their yards or kitchens (with the curtains drawn), then put on their Sunday best and searched for hymnbooks and Bibles neglected during the rest of the week. They put on tight patent-leather shoes, had a hurried breakfast of hot coffee and koeksisters, and walked wincingly up Caledon Street to attend the morning service at St. Mark's. Those less virtuous tossed dreamlessly, fading out the monotony of the week before at the same job in the same factory for the same wages which were never enough for groceries and rent and a bit of booze and maybe an evening with the girls at Mary's.

At midday we were served with the heaviest meal of the week. We sat around the dining-room table stiff and uncomfortable in our navy-blue best. After a long drawn-out grace we started with curry and yellow rice rich with raisins and cinnamon. The curry was pale and anemic because my aunt, who always lunched with us on Sundays, claimed to suffer from acid winds. But after that we had thick slices of roast and potatoes smothered in gravy, and red beetroot salad. And finally jelly and custard and sometimes bread or rice pudding.

In the afternoon, when the adults were snoring heavily, we children would roam the streets, always careful not to soil our Sunday suits. On rare occasions we ventured downtown to the Museum to see the models of Bushmen with big bums or furtively glance at the nude statues in the Art Galleries. What a wicked and enjoyable place the world was. What goings-on. And then we walked back through the Botanical Gardens whooping and shouting and raising havoc deliberately to frighten fragile little white ladies sitting on quiet benches, who would then complain to the attendants about those rude slum children.

Back home the darkness descended from Table Mountain and the streetlamps flickered to life at the tops of their stalks, leaving pools of light at their bases in which we played our games till called inside because it was school tomorrow. It was always school tomorrow on Sunday evenings when we were enjoying ourselves, even when we knew it was vacation time. The hush crept over the District as one by one the lights were switched off or paraffin lamps blown out until there was only the basin of darkness at the foot of the mountain illumined by rows of lamppost stalks. The streets would empty until in the small hours there were only stray dogs, prowling cats, solitary drunks and hawkers' carts leaning awkwardly with their long shafts against the walls.

And I still clearly remember the characters and the incidents.

Age of Iron

J. M. Coetzee

IN THE SMALL HOURS of last night there was a telephone call. A woman, breathless, with the breathlessness of fat people. "I want to speak to Florence."

"She is sleeping. Everyone is sleeping."

"Yes, you can call her."

It was raining, though not hard. I knocked at Florence's door. At once it opened, as if she had been standing there waiting for the summons. From behind her came the sleepy groan of a child. "Telephone," I said.

Five minutes later she came up to my room. Without her glasses, bareheaded, in a long white nightdress, she seemed much younger.

"There is trouble," she said.

"Is it Bheki?"

"Yes, I must go."

J. M. COETZEE (1940–). A novelist, critic, and translator, Coetzee won the Nobel Prize in 2003 and twice claimed the Booker Prize. His prose is sometimes referred to as steely, but below the apparently uncomplicated surface is always a challenging philosophical undercurrent. This excerpt is from the novel of the same title.

"Where is he?"

"First I must go to Guguletu, then after that, I think, to Site C."

"I have no idea where Site C is."

She gave me a puzzled look.

"I mean, if you can show me the way I will take you by car," I said.

"Yes," she said, but still hesitated. "But I cannot leave the children alone."

"Then they must come along."

"Yes," she said. I could not remember ever seeing her so indecisive.

. . .

With the two children on the back seat warmly covered, Florence pushed. We set off. Peering through glass misted over with our breathing, I crawled over De Waal Drive, got lost for a while in the streets of Claremont, then found Lansdowne Road. The first buses of the day were abroad, brightly lit and empty. It was not yet five o'clock.

We passed the last houses, the last streetlights. Into a steady rain from the northwest we drove, following the faint yellow glow of our headlights.

"If people wave to you to stop, or if you see things in the road, you must not stop, you must drive on," said Florence.

"I will certainly not," I said. "You should have warned me earlier. Let me make myself clear, Florence, at the first sign of trouble I am turning back."

"I do not say it will happen, I am just telling you."

Full of misgiving I drove on into the darkness. But no one barred the way, no one waved, there was nothing across the road. Trouble, it seemed, was still in bed; trouble was recuperating for the next engagement. The roadside, along which, at this hour, thousands of men would ordinarily have been plodding to work, was empty. Swirls of mist floated toward us, embraced the car, floated away. Wraiths, spirits. Aornos this place: birdless. I shivered, met Florence's gaze. "How much farther?" I asked.

"Not far."

"What did they say on the telephone?"

"They were shooting again yesterday. They were giving guns to the *witdoeke* and the *witdoeke* were shooting."

"Are they shooting in Guguletu?"

"No, they are shooting out in the bush."

"At the first hint of trouble, Florence, I am turning back. We are fetching Bheki, that is all we are going to do, then we are going home. You should never have let him leave."

"Yes, but you must turn here, you must turn left."

I turned. A hundred meters farther there was a barrier across the road with flashing lights, cars parked along the verges, police with guns. I stopped; a policeman came up.

"What is your business here?" he asked.

"I am taking my domestic home," I said, surprised at how calmly I lied.

He peered at the children sleeping on the back seat. "Where does she live?"

"Fifty-seven," said Florence.

"You can drop her here, she can walk, it is not far."

"It is raining, she has small children, I am not letting her walk alone," I said firmly.

He hesitated, then with his flashlight waved me through. On the roof of one of the cars stood a young man in battle-dress, his gun at the ready, staring out into the darkness.

Now there was a smell of burning in the air, of wet ash, burning rubber. Slowly we drove down a broad unpaved street lined with matchbox-houses. A police van armored in wire mesh cruised past us. "Turn right here," said Florence. "Turn right again. Stop here."

With the baby on her arm and the little girl, only half awake, stumbling behind, she splashed up the path to No. 219, knocked, was admitted. Hope and Beauty. It was like living in an allegory. Keeping the engine running, I waited.

The police van that had passed us drew up alongside. A light shone in my face. I held up a hand to shield my eyes. The van pulled away.

Florence re-emerged holding a plastic raincoat over herself and the baby, and got into the back seat. Dashing through the rain behind her came not Bheki but a man in his thirties or forties, slight, dapper, with a mustache. He got in beside me. "This is Mr. Thabane my cousin," said Florence. "He will show us the way."

"Where is Hope?" I asked.

"I have left her with my sister."

"And where is Bheki?"

There was silence.

"I am not sure," said the man. His voice was surprisingly soft. "He came in yesterday morning and put his things down and went out. After that we did not see him at all. He did not come home to sleep. But I know where his friends live. We can start looking there."

"Is this what you want, Florence?" I asked.

"We must look for him," said Florence: "there is nothing else we can do."

"If you would prefer me to drive I can drive," said the man. "It is anyhow better, you know."

I got out and sat beside Florence in the back. The rain was coming down more heavily now; the car splashed through pools on the uneven road. Left and right we turned under the sick orange of the streetlights, then stopped. "Careful, don't switch off," I said to Mr. Thabane the cousin.

He got out and knocked at a window. A long conversation followed with someone I could not see. By the time he came back he was soaked and cold. With clumsy fingers he took out a pack of cigarettes and tried to light one. "Please, not in the car," I said. A look of exasperation passed between him and Florence.

We sat in silence. "What are we waiting for?" I asked.

"They are sending someone to show us the way."

A little boy wearing a balaclava cap too large for him came trotting out of the house. With entire self-assurance, greeting us all with a smile, he got into the car and began to give directions. Ten years old at most. A child of the times, at home in this landscape of violence. When I think back to my own childhood I remember only long sun-struck afternoons, the smell of dust under avenues of eucalyptus, the quiet rustle of water in roadside furrows, the lulling of doves. A childhood of sleep, prelude to what was meant to be a life without trouble and a smooth passage to Nirvana. Will we at least be allowed our Nirvana, we children of that bygone age? I doubt it. If justice reigns at all, we will find ourselves barred at the first threshold of the underworld. White as grubs in our swaddling bands, we will be dispatched to join those infant souls whose eternal whining Aeneas mistook for weeping. White our color, the color of limbo: white sands, white rocks, a white light pouring down from all sides. Like an eternity of lying on the beach, an endless Sunday among thousands of our own kind, sluggish, half asleep, in earshot of the comfortable lap of the waves. *In limine primo:* on the threshold of death, the threshold of life. Creatures thrown up by the sea, stalled on the sands, undecided, indecisive, neither hot nor cold, neither fish nor fowl.

We had passed the last of the houses and were driving in gray early-morning light through a landscape of scorched earth, blackened trees. A pickup truck passed us with three men in the back sheltering under a tarpaulin. At the next road-block we caught up with them again. They gazed expressionlessly at us, eye to eye, as we waited to be inspected. A policeman waved them through, waved us through too.

We turned north, away from the mountain, then off the highway on to a dirt road that soon became sand. Mr. Thabane stopped. "We can't drive farther, it is too dangerous," he said. "There is something wrong with your alternator," he added, pointing to the red light glowing on the dashboard.

"I am letting things run down," I said. I did not feel like explaining.

He switched off the engine. For a while we sat listening to the rain drumming on the roof. Then Florence got out, and the boy. Tied on her back, the baby slept peacefully.

"It is best if you keep the doors locked," said Mr. Thabane to me.

"How long will you be?"

"I cannot say, but we will hurry."

I shook my head. "I am not staying here," I said.

I had no hat, no umbrella. The rain beat against my face, pasted my hair to my scalp, ran down my neck. From this sort of outing, I thought, one catches one's death of cold. The boy, our guide, had already dashed ahead.

"Put this over your head," said Mr. Thabane, offering the plastic raincoat.

"Nonsense," I said, "I don't mind a little rain."

"Still, hold it over you," he insisted. I understood. "Come," he said. I followed.

Around us was a wilderness of gray dune-sand and Port Jackson willow, and a stench of garbage and ash. Shreds of plastic, old iron, glass, animal bones littered both sides of the path. I was already shivering with cold, but when I tried to walk faster my heart pounded unpleasantly. I was falling behind. Would Florence pause? No: *amor matris*, a force that stopped for nothing.

At a fork in the path Mr. Thabane was waiting. "Thank you," I gasped, "you are kind. I am sorry to be holding you up. I have a bad hip."

"Take my arm," he said.

Men passed us, dark, bearded, stern, armed with sticks, walking swiftly in single file. Mr. Thabane stepped off the path. I held tighter to him.

The path widened, then came to an end in a wide, flat pond. On the far side of the pond the shanties started, the lowest-lying cluster surrounded by water, flooded. Some built sturdily of wood and iron, others no more than skins of plastic sheeting over frames of branches, they straggled north over the dunes as far as I could see.

At the brink of the pond I hesitated. "Come," said Mr. Thabane. Holding on to him I stepped in, and we waded across, in water up to our ankles. One of my shoes was sucked off. "Watch out for broken glass," he warned. I retrieved the shoe.

Save for an old woman with a sagging mouth standing in a doorway, there was no one in sight. But as we walked farther the noise we had heard, which at first might have been taken for wind and rain, began to break up into shouts, cries, calls, over a ground-bass which I can only call a sigh: a deep sigh, repeated over and over, as if the wide world itself were sighing.

Then the little boy, our guide, was with us again, tugging Mr. Thabane's sleeve, talking excitedly. The two of them broke away; I struggled behind them up the dune side.

We were at the rear of a crowd hundreds strong looking down upon a scene of devastation: shanties burnt and smoldering, shanties still burning, pouring forth black smoke. Jumbles of furniture, bedding, household objects stood in the pouring rain. Gangs of men were at work trying to rescue the contents of the burning shacks, going from one to another, putting out the fires; or so I thought till with a shock it came to me that these were no rescuers but incendiaries, that the battle I saw them waging was not with the flames but with the rain.

It was from the people gathered on the rim of this amphitheater in the dunes that the sighing came. Like mourners at a funeral they stood in the downpour, men, women and children, sodden, hardly bothering to protect themselves, watching the destruction.

Krot

Rustum Kozain

"*KROT*," JACOB SAID OUT LOUD to himself. Then, half muttering, half thinking: "I live in a *krot*."

He wondered for a moment at that word, the consonants coming together quickly despite the vowel, which opened briefly like a dark mouth, then snapped shut. The scratch of the "kr" stopping short on the "t," like a cockroach startled and scuttling across the floor, disappearing behind a shelf or under a chair.

For months, dishes had been piling up, scraps of food shrivelling, dregs of coffee and tea growing mold in mugs, a sliver of cheese sweating until it shone like plastic. There were stacks of books and unread newspapers everywhere— not only in the study, but also in the bathroom, the bedroom, on the coffee table in the lounge, and in stacks on the floors. Over some single pages left where they had slipped from the coffee table, ran a cheerful silver trail

RUSTUM KOZAIN (1966–), born and raised in Paarl, Western Cape, studied English literature and lectured at the University of Cape Town. His debut collection of poetry, *This Carting Life* (2005), was awarded the Ingrid Jonker Prize in 2006 and the Olive Schreiner Prize in 2007. *Krot* is a work in progress.

where a snail had crawled, but otherwise everything had a crust of grime. Occasionally, the green leaves and purple flowers from the monstrous bougainvillaea outside, blown in through the gap underneath the kitchen door, also brought an unusual cheer into the house.

"Breaking down the boundary between nature and civilization," Jacob sometimes had joked to friends in lighter times.

Soon, though, the leaves and flowers would shrivel and gather a patina of dust. Even the cobwebs—impressive architectures with tunnels and spanning the corners of the ceilings—were dark with dust. In some of these were caught the husks of spiders and their insect prey. In the passage lay a few dead cockroaches, hunted by the cat and left there to dry. And fleas had also now established their colonies. If he tarried anywhere dusty, Jacob was sure to feel a bite.

No part of the house was in any order, so that no matter which part of the house he was in, the disorder was always there, persistent like the confusing memories of a nightmare at the back of the head.

It held him down, but his habits had for two years now strayed from order. Sometimes, when Jacob handed out dinner invitations on a drunken whim, he strained himself to clean and tidy the house. On these occasions, he managed to pull it into some shape, and could host a small dinner party without too much fear of shame or embarrassment at the rickety, dusty house he managed to rent. If he gave himself enough time, he could usually tidy the whole place, study and desk included. But some tension never disappeared, until after a dinner party, when, within a week, the house would descend back into its chaos as he himself relaxed back into himself, doing nothing but holding out against the slow but definite run of time.

It was clear to Jacob himself that the state of the house was related to the state of his mind, although his mind wasn't in disorder. Neither had his mind become slothful. But it was as if the house and his mind had joined forces, shutting close—not shutting *out*, as his house may have shut out order, but, like his mind, not staying open to others, not welcoming scrutiny. It was his mind that disliked others wandering in, asking questions which he either had not resolved or refused to resolve. Though he enjoyed company, for the past two years he had slowly started to withdraw, except to socialize with a small group of people. But not at his house.

Thoughts of the disorder exhausted him as much as thoughts about his life.

Sometimes he felt as if the house were alive, growing slowly, a large malevolence that was starting to incorporate the disorder. When he returned from brief errands, a slight, fetid smell could be discerned when opening the front door, as if an entity, part vegetable, part flesh, had woken and been eructating somewhere at the back.

$\sim$

In the mirror when he shaved was a man he sometimes remembered. But most of the time the image was unrecognizable. The teeth going, the pouch beneath the chin, the dark stains of aging forming on his skin. When he turned away to reach for the hand towel, he saw a small hump on his back, on the right shoulder blade. Or turning back to face himself in the mirror, he saw a man with a long chin and buck teeth.

Leaving the bathroom, or closing a wardrobe door, he caught the flutter of his reflection in the mirrors, indistinct and glimpsed from the corner of his eye, a moth-like remnant of conscience.

Given the light scowl on his face when he left his house for the streets of his neighborhood, and the slight hunch of his shoulders, he may as well have carried a hump; his smile, if there were to be one, may as well have split his face and revealed the teeth of a monster. All he felt was the wish not to be seen and the wish for the tension of the mask he had to wear to dissolve.

The narrow road was narrower for cars parked on either side and for the double row of small houses of which his was one. Despite a few colorful ones, despite individual renovations and modifications done by owners, the houses could not break from the conformity and the efficiency of past town planners. And the houses, in their persistent, foundational sameness, reminded him of a set of teeth. Growth from irregularity to evenness, until the growth gave way, falling back onto an irregular pattern and regression.

The inevitable wind of summer blew around scraps of grimy litter and leaves, across the street, in the gutters, strewing the pavement: a styrofoam box from a fast-food dinner, an empty chips packet, a catalogue for cheap electronics. A patch of broken glass on the pavement where sometime last night a car was burgled. Behind a high fence and electric gate, the empty parking lot of an aban-

doned small business, strewn with the cracked plastic of
discarded computers, a stainless steel sink, and a street
cat prowling and sniffing. A few steps away from a stool
of dry, gray dog shit, a drunk, homeless man was sleeping
on the pavement, tethered to his shopping cart, dressed in
tattered, rank, piss-stained clothes, grubby toes sticking
out from the rags swaddled around his feet. He moaned
in his sleep.

Fifty meters or so from there was the main road through
the neighborhood. The late-afternoon, homeward-bound
traffic was increasing and cars filled with impatient office
workers, trucks and bakkies filled with the ghosts of
workers—some of whom burst into life at the sight of a
young woman on the pavement—crawled along the road.
Workers from construction sites, nurses from the hospital
close by, and a miscellany of people rushed in talkative
groups down pavement routes leading to the train station
a few blocks from the main road. For two blocks north to
south along the main road, around a small central area
of the neighborhood, a number of bars and restaurants
and a miscellany of hairdressers, a book store, bottle store,
and so on formed a hub that came alive from late afternoon onward, growing noisily at night and closing in the
early hours of the morning with loud, drunken voices, the
screech of tires, or the roar of a motorcycle. A nightlife
after its scruffy nature, now already filling the streets with
mostly young people dressed in an assortment of ragged,
recycled fashions.

Coming from his darkened house in which he hid most
of the day, frittering away the hours doing this or that,
reading a paragraph or two of a book that would be another

false start, cleaning just enough utensils for a sandwich at lunch or for the gluttonous meal later that night, starting at a piece of work but faltering soon enough, he walked down the road with a sense of brief elation. Elation to feel the last of the sun on his face, to see the world alive with people and activity, but brief because it gave way almost instantly to resentment—a resentment that he had somehow allowed himself to miss, again, a day. That somehow he could live so that he could feel part of all this. Not as a fellow party-goer, but that he could feel less hurried at the end of the day that he had once again let slip through his fingers and which he was now trying to redeem: hurrying to the supermarket to buy some food and cigarettes, hurrying back home to disappear again into his house and try and do something that would truly postpone the inexorable drive of time. Something. Some work, read a book. Or even visit a friend. But at the back of his head was the idea of pressure he kept alive so that he was always working, so that there was never enough time. And hurrying because he *was* hiding, scared that someone would recognize that no matter the insistence on the pressures of work and time, he was a hollow man and thus could be invisible.

The Turban

A. C. Jordan

IT CAME ABOUT, according to some tale, that there was a man named Nyengebule. This man had two wives, and of these two, it was only the head wife who bore him children. But Nyengebule's *ntandanekazi* (favorite wife) was the junior one, because she was younger, livelier, and more attractive than the head wife. Nyengebule's in-laws by the junior wife were very fond of him, all of them. He was a warm-hearted and generous man. The women especially—his sisters-in-law including his wife's brothers' wives—used to be delighted when he paid them a visit. They would crowd round him and listen to the amusing stories he had to tell and also to demand the gifts to which they were entitled. These Nyengebule never failed to bring, but because he knew he was the favorite *mkhwenyethu* (brother-in-law), he delighted in teasing the women before producing the gifts, pretending he

A. C. JORDAN (1906–1968) was a linguist, literary critic, novelist, professor of Bantu languages, and cricket player. His novel *Ingqumbo yeMinyanya* (The Wrath of the Ancestors), published in 1940, has been hailed the finest novel written in Xhosa.

had not brought them any gifts because he had had to leave home at short notice, or because he had lost the bag that contained them on his way, or because his wife had offended him in one way or another just before he left home, and he had decided to punish her by not bringing her people any gifts. Then he would sit listening and smiling as the women coaxed and cajoled him, calling him by the great praises of his clan and by his personal ones. But in the end the gifts always came out, each one of them accompanied by an appropriate spoken message of flattery to the receiver. Nyengebule was very popular with the friends and neighbors of his in-laws too, because he was a great entertainer, a great leader of song and dance. Whenever there was a *mgidi* (festival) at his in-laws, the whole neighborhood used to look forward to his coming, because things became lively as soon as he arrived.

Nyengebule's in-laws were sad that their daughter could not bear this man children. In the early years of this marriage, they tried everything they could to doctor her, and when they were convinced that she was barren, they suggested that one of the younger sisters should be taken in marriage by Nyengebule so that she could bear children for her sister. Nyengebule's own people supported this and urged him, reminding him that, by virtue of the *khazi* (bride-tribute) he had already given for the woman who turned out to be barren, he could marry one of the younger sisters without giving any more cattle. But Nyengebule kept on putting this off. To his own people he stated quite openly that he did not desire to do such a thing, that he did not see the need for it because he had enough children by his head wife, and because he loved his junior wife even though she bore him no children. To his senior in-laws he spoke more tactfully, because he knew that it would hurt them if he stated that it made no difference to him whether or not there were children by his marriage with their daughter. So he asked them to give him time. With his brothers-in-law he treated the matter as a joke.

"Oh, get away, you fellows!" he said on one occasion. "I know you will be the first to hate me if I do this, because it will deprive you of the opportunity to extort cattle from some other fellow who would have to give some cattle for the girl you offer me."

Everyone present laughed at this. But one of the senior brothers-in-law pressed him. Then Nyengebule said he wanted time to decide which one of his growing sisters-in-law would get on well with his wife as a co-wife. But when the girls he promised to choose from reached marriageable age, he had some other excuse for his delay. At last there came a time when the in-laws decided never to raise the matter again. Nyengebule was happy with their daughter, and the best thing to do was to leave it to these two to raise the matter, if and when they should desire such an arrangement.

One day, there came an invitation to Nyengebule and his junior wife. There was going to be a great festival at his in-laws on such and such a day, and he was being invited to be present with his wife. With great delight these two made all the necessary preparations. Two days before the day of departure, it occurred to the wife that on her return from these festivities she would be too tired to go gathering firewood, and that it would be wise to gather sufficient wood now, to last her some time after her return. She mentioned this to her co-wife, who decided she might as well go and gather some wood too.

The two women left home early the following morning. When they entered the woods, they separated, each one taking her own direction to find, cut, and pick dry wood and pile it to make her own bundle. But they kept in touch all the time, ever calling to each other to find out if things were going well. The final calls came when each one thought her bundle was big enough, and the two came together to sit and rest before carrying the firewood home. This was early in the afternoon.

While they were sitting there, there was a chirrup! chirrup! The junior wife was the first to hear it and she immediately recognized it as the call of the honeybird. She looked about, and saw this tiny bird fluttering about, now toward her, now away from her, and then toward her and away again.

"The honeybird!" she said and sprang up to follow it.

The honeybird led her on and on, chirrupping as it went, until it came to a bees' nest. As soon as she saw this the woman called out to tell her co-wife what she had "discovered." The head wife came immediately, and the two gathered the honeycombs and piled them on a patch of green grass while the honeybird fluttered about hopefully. When they had finished, they picked up all the honey, except one comb that they left for the bird, and returned to the place where they had left their bundles of wood, and they sat down and ate together.

As they ate, the head wife took two pieces at a time, ate one and laid the other aside. She did this until they finished. It was only when she saw the head wife packing together what she had been laying aside that the junior wife became aware of what had been happening.

"Oh!" she said. "I didn't think of that. Why didn't you tell me to put some aside too?"

In reply the head wife said, "You know why you didn't think of it? It's because you have no children. It's only a woman who has children who remembers that she must lay something aside as she eats."

The junior wife made no reply to this, and the two picked up their bundles and carried them home.

Nyengebule had been busy all day setting things in order. As far as his side of the preparations was concerned, everything that he intended to take with him to this festival was ready. Even the large fat gelded goat he was going to give as a son-in-law's customary contribution to the festival had already been chosen and fastened to the gatepost, so that it should be ready to lead away the following morning. Now he was waiting until his wives returned so that he should announce to his head wife formally that he and the junior wife would leave at cockcrow, and also to give orders to his boys as to what had to be done by this one and by that one while he was away.

As soon as his wives had entered their respective houses and seen to the few things that usually need straightening up when a wife has been away from her house the whole day, Nyengebule went to the house of his head wife and made this announcement and gave the orders to the boys. His head wife listened very carefully as he gave orders to the boys, and when he had finished, she went over them all, taking one boy after the other:

"Have you heard then, So-and-so? Your father wants you to do this and that while he is away. And you, So-and-so, have you heard what your father says? He wants you to do this, and this, and that."

After this, she brought out the honey. She took some combs and served them up to her husband in a plate made of clay, and the rest she gave to her children.

"So you women discovered bees today!" said Nyengebule as he gratefully received his share.

"Yes," said his head wife. "It was *Nobani* (So-and-so) who discovered them. She was drawn by the honeybird."

"Well done!" said Nyengebule. "But aren't you going to have any yourself?"

"No, thank you. I had enough in the woods."

So Nyengebule ate his share and finished it. Then, thanking his head wife for the honey, he said good-bye to them all and went to the junior house. He was looking forward to a much bigger feast of honey. If his head wife had so much to give him, certainly his *ntandanekazi* must have laid aside much more for him, especially as it was she who had "discovered." There were no children to share the honey with, and he and his *ntandanekazi* would enjoy the honey together, just the two of them.

He found his junior wife busy with her packing. The evening meal was not yet ready. Nyengebule did not say anything about the honey, because he thought his *ntandanekazi* wanted to give him a pleasant surprise. Maybe she would produce the honey just before the evening meal. But when the food was ready, his wife served it up to him and said nothing about the honey. After the meal, she removed the dishes and washed them and put them away. Now, surely, the honey was coming? But the woman resumed her packing, paying particular attention to each ornament before deciding whether to take it with her or not. She would pick this one up and add it to her luggage, and then replace it by another one. Now and again she would find something wrong with the beads of this or that necklace and pull them out and reset them. She would dig out some ornament that she had not worn for a long time and compare it with one that she had acquired recently, taking long to make up her mind which one was more suitable than the other for this occasion. This went on and on until everyone else had gone to sleep and the whole village was quiet.

When at last she was satisfied that her luggage contained everything she would require for the festivities, the woman yawned and looked at her husband.

"I think we had better sleep now if we mean to leave at cockcrow," she said.

"Sleep? Isn't there something you've forgotten to give me?"

"Something to give you?"

"Yes! Where's all the honey you brought me?"

"I didn't bring you any honey."

"You're playing!"

"In truth, I didn't bring you any honey. If you think I'm playing, look for yourself. I forgot really."

"You forgot? You forgot *me*? What is it that you remember then, if you forget *me*?"

Before she could reply, Nyengebule grabbed a heavy stick and in his anger he struck her hard. The blow landed on her left temple, and she fell to the ground. Terrified at this sight, Nyengebule flung the stick away and ran across the hut and bent over her body, calling her softly by name. Weakly her eyes opened, and then they closed, never to open again.

Nyengebule burst out of the hut, his first impulse being to shout for help, but no sooner had he run out than he retreated into the hut on tiptoe, frightened by the peace and silence of the night. He knelt by his wife's body and touched her here, here, and there. Dead! His *ntandanekazi* dead? Yes, quite dead! What is he going to do? He cannot call anyone in here now. He must bury her before dawn. Yes, he must bury her alone. He is lucky too that everyone knows that he should be away at cockcrow. He must bury her and leave at cockcrow as arranged. Then his head wife and the children and all the neighbors will think she has gone with him.

He took a shovel and a long digging-rod and crept out to dig the grave. When he had finished he returned to the hut and looked around. That luggage! That luggage of his wife's! That must be buried with her. He carried the woman's body and laid it in the grave. Then he brought the luggage and laid it beside her body. He covered the body with earth and removed every trace he could find of this night's happenings. But there was one thing he had not noticed. The turban his wife had been wearing that evening had dropped on the ground between the house and the grave.

Nyengebule returned to his house, but not to sleep. What must he do now? Can he still go to his in-laws? Yes, that he must, because if he and his wife do not turn up, the in-laws will know there's something wrong and send someone to come and see what it is. But he has never gone to such festivities alone. His wife has always gone with him. How is he going to explain her absence this time? It will not sound good to his in-laws to say their daughter is ill, for how could he leave her alone then? What is more, they might do what they have always done when their daughter was reported ill—send one of her younger sisters to come and look after her and her husband. But go he must, for this is the only way he can find time to decide what to do. He will leave at cockcrow as arranged. Then he will try to be as he has always been until the festivities are over. Then what? Then what?

"Kurukuku-u-u-u-ku" crowed the cocks. Nyengebule crept out of bed and picked up his bags. He tiptoed out of the hut and fastened the door. He spoke softly to the goat as he approached it, in case it should make a noise and rouse his dogs as well as those of his neighbors. But the goat did not give him the least trouble. It was willing to be unfastened and led away.

Nyengebule traveled fast, like one who was running away from something. The goat did not handicap him because his boys had trained it for purposes of riding. Sometimes he led it by the rope, and sometimes he drove it before him.

Early in the afternoon, he had to leave the straight road by which he had been traveling most of the time and take a turn, walking along a path that led straight to his in-laws. Nyengebule stood for a while at this point, undecided whether to take the turn to his in-laws or continue along the straight road, going he knew not where. At last he took the turn. He had taken only a few paces when a honeybird appeared. It fluttered a little ahead of him and led him the way he was going but the calls it made were not those that a honeybird makes when it leads a person to a bees' nest:

uNyongenul' uyibulel' *intandanekazi,*	Nyengebule has killed his favorite wife,
Ibonisel' iinyosi, yaphakula, *Yatya, yalibal' ukumbekela;*	She discovered bees and gathered the honey,
Uyiselele kunye nezivatho *zomgidi,*	She ate and forgot to leave him a share;
Akasibon' isankwane sisiw' *endleleni.*	He buried her together with her festival dress,
	And saw not the turban dropping on the way.

Nyengebule was startled. Did these words really come from that bird? And where had this bird gone to now? It had vanished. He went on. The bird appeared again and repeated its actions and song, but before he could do anything about it, it had vanished. But now he made up his mind what to do if it could come again. He would throw a stick at it and kill it. The honeybird appeared a third time and repeated its actions and song. Nyengebule let fly his stick and hit it, breaking one of its wings. The bird vanished, but the broken wing fluttered a little and then fell at his feet, no longer a honeybird's wing but the turban worn by his wife the time he killed her.

He let it lie there for a while and stood looking at it. His *ntandanekazi's* turban! Can he leave it there? It should have been buried with her. He must keep it until he can find an opportunity to do this. He picked it up and put it into the bag that contained gifts for his in-laws.

As soon as he came in sight of his in-laws', the married women came out to welcome him with the shrills and ululations that announce the arrival of anyone who comes driving an animal for slaughter to such festivals. As soon as Nyengebule reached the *nkundla* (courtyard), his brothers-in-law relieved him of the goat, and their wives continued to sing his people's praises as they led him to the hut set aside for him and his wife. In no time, the sisters-in-law came crowding in this hut.

"But where's our sister?" they asked.

"So she hasn't arrived yet?" asked Nyengebule.

"No, she hasn't arrived. When did she leave home?"

"I left a little earlier than she because of the goat I had to bring with me. But she was almost ready when I left and I thought she would be here before me because she was going to take a short cut and wasn't handicapped like me. She should be here soon."

They brought him water so that he could wash, and immediately after, some food and beer to make him the jolly *mkhwenyethu* they knew he could be.

The festival was to open on the following day, and therefore the in-laws and their closest friends were busy with the final preparations. The women were straining those quantities of beer that must be ready for the next day, and the men were chopping wood and slaughtering oxen and goats. All the people working at these assignments were already keyed up for the festival. There was plenty of meat and beer for them, and there were far more people than work to do. Therefore most of them were practicing the

songs and dances with which they intended to impress
the guests expected. Nyengebule's arrival therefore caused
a great deal of excitement. Now that he had come, they
could be sure that they would more than measure up to
the famous expert singers and dancers with whom they
would have to compete during these festivities. They were
sure that this great singer and dancer had added something to his store since they last met him, and they were
eager to learn these new things before "that great day of
tomorrow." So, even before Nyengebule had finished eating and drinking, there were loud, impatient calls from his
brothers-in-law and their friends to the *mkhwe* to "come
to the men." But his sisters-in-law were not prepared to
let him go until they had fed him and until they knew
what gifts he had brought them. For some of these gifts
might be dainty ornaments that would just be suitable for
the festivites.

At last, two of his brothers-in-law went to him.

"On your feet, *mkhwe!*" they said. "These wives and
sisters of ours can get their gifts later. Get up and come
to the men."

So saying, they lifted him up and carried him away,
amid the amused protests of his sisters-in-law, as against
the shouts of triumph from the onlookers to whom
Nyengebule was being carried. As soon as he arrived,
the men greeted him with his praises and with song and
dance, and invited him to join them. Many of the less
busy women in the courtyard cheered, and in no time the
place was crowded with onlookers of all ages.

The sisters-in-law, however, remained in the hut, more
curious to know what gifts they were getting than to join

the admiring crowds. "I wonder what gift he has brought me this time, and what naughty things he is going to say when he gives it to me!" thought each one. After all, he was their favorite *mkhwenyethu*, and if he should discover at some time that while he was dancing in the courtyard they opened the bag of gifts just to have a look, of course he would pretend to be offended, but in fact he would be delighted. So thought the sisters-in-law, and they pulled out the bag of gifts and opened it. When a little bird's wing flew out of the bag and fluttered above their heads toward the roof, there were screams of delight, for everyone thought this was just one of the *mkhwenyethu's* endless pranks. But the next moment, the women huddled together, horrified by the song of the honeybird:

> *Nyengebule has killed his favorite wife;*
> *She discovered bees and gathered honey,*
> *She ate and forgot to leave him a share;*
> *He buried her together with her festival clothes*
> *And saw not the turban she dropped on the way.*

The women watched the wing speechlessly as it came down, down, down, until it landed on the floor and became a turban that they all knew very well.

Shouts and cheers in the courtyard! Shrills and ululations in the courtyard! Hand-clapping, song, and drums in the courtyard! Admiration and praises for Nyengebule in the courtyard! Few of the onlookers, and none of the dancers, have noticed that the sons of this house—Nyengebule's brothers-in-law and their cousins—were quietly being called away, one by one, from this rejoicing. To the few who have noticed this, nothing is unusual about *imilowo* (those of the family) occasionally with-drawing quietly to hold council about the running of a big festival of this nature.

Nyengebule was just beginning to teach a new song when two of his in-laws' elderly neighbors came to tell him that he was wanted by his in-laws. Up to this moment, he had not met his parents-in-law, and he assumed that he was being requested to go to the great hut and pre-sent himself formally. But when he indicated to the two elders that he would have to go to his hut and change his dress before meeting his parents-in-law, one of them said, "There's no need for that. It's over there that you are wanted." The elder was pointing higher up the slope, to an old, high-walled stone building—the most prominent building among the ruins of what used to be the home of the forebears of Nyengebule's in-laws.

The elders walked a few paces alongside him and then they stopped and once again pointed out the building to which he had to go. Who wanted him? he wondered. Maybe his brothers-in-law needed his help about some-thing or other? Maybe they expected so many guests that they thought they could prepare this old building for the overflow? But when he reached the door, the place was so quiet that he did not expect to find anyone inside.

He pushed the door open without knocking, and he felt cold in the stomach when he entered. Here were all his in-laws—his parents-in-law, his wife's father's broth-ers and their wives, his wife's father's sisters and their husbands, his wife's mother's brothers and their wives, his wife's mother's sisters and their husbands, his brothers-in-law and their wives, his wife's cousins and their wives or husbands, his sisters-in-law—all of them standing, silent, solemn. In the center of the building there was a newly dug grave. On the piles of earth that came out of the grave was the bag containing the gifts he had brought his sisters-in-law. Next to this lay the body of the large fat gelded goat he had brought as his contribution to the festival. No one acknowledged his hoarse, half-whispered greetings. Instead, his father-in-law pointed a finger at the bag of gifts.

"Open that," was all he said.

Nyengebule lifted up the bag and opened it, but he dropped it again, his knees sagging a little. The wing of the honeybird had flown out and was fluttering above the heads of those present, singing its song. When it finished, it dropped at Nyengebule's feet and became his dead wife's turban. Nyengebule gave it one look and then raised his head to look at his father-in-law for the next order. But the father-in-law turned his face away from him and signaled his eldest sister, a married woman. She stepped forward, lifted the bag of gifts, and cast it into the grave. The father-in-law signaled his two eldest sons. They stepped forward, lifted the dead goat, and cast it into the grave. Once more the father-in-law signaled, and this time all his sons and brother's sons stepped forward and closed in on Nyengebule. All the women covered their faces, but the men looked on grimly, noting every little detail of what was happening. They noted with silent admiration that Nyengebule did not shudder when these men laid their hands on him. They noted that he did not struggle or try to resist when they laid him down on the floor, face down. They noted that he did not wince when some of the men bound his feet together and sat on his legs, while others stretched out his arms sideways and sat on them. They noted that he did not groan when his two senior brothers-in-law raised his head and twisted his neck.

Four men jumped into the grave and stood ready to receive his limp body from their kinsmen. Everyone was looking now. As the four men laid him carefully on his back beside his rejected gifts, everyone saw the wing of the honeybird fluttering over the grave. As soon as the four men had done their solemn duty and climbed out of the grave, everyone saw the wing of the honeybird landing on the chest of the dying man and becoming his dead wife's turban. Everyone saw Nyengebule's arms moving weakly and rising slowly, slowly, slowly from his sides to his chest. The women sobbed when they saw his hands closing on the turban and pressing it to his heart.

His brothers-in-law and their cousins brought shovels and took their places round the grave. They lifted their first shovelfuls, but before throwing the earth onto his motionless body, they paused just for one moment and bowed their heads, for they noticed that the turban was still pressed to the heart of the dead man.

1899

Olive Schreiner

Thou fool, that which thou sowest
is not quickened unless it die.

I

IT WAS A WARM NIGHT: the stars shone down through
the thick soft air of the Northern Transvaal into the dark
earth, where a little daub-and-wattle house of two rooms
lay among the long, grassy slopes.

A light shone through the small window of the house,
though it was past midnight. Presently the upper half of
the door opened and then the lower, and the tall figure
of a woman stepped out into the darkness. She closed
the door behind her and walked toward the back of the
house where a large round hut stood; beside it lay a pile
of stumps and branches quite visible when once the eyes
grew accustomed to the darkness. The woman stooped
and broke off twigs till she had her apron full, and then
returned slowly, and went into the house.

OLIVE SCHREINER (1855–1920) is best known for her novel
The Story of an African Farm. A pacifist, defender of women's
suffrage, and important feminist thinker, Schreiner supported
the Afrikaners against the British in the Anglo-Boer War and
later the Africans against both.

The room to which she returned was a small, bare room, with brown earthen walls and a mud floor; a naked deal table stood in the center, and a few dark wooden chairs, homemade, with seats of undressed leather, stood round the walls. In the corner opposite the door was an open fireplace; and on the earthen hearth stood an iron three-foot, on which stood a large black kettle, under which coals were smoldering, though the night was hot and close. Against the wall on the left side of the room hung a gun rack with three guns upon it, and below it a large hunting watch hung from two nails by its silver chain.

In the corner by the fireplace was a little table with a coffeepot upon it and a dish containing cups and saucers covered with water, and above it were a few shelves with crockery and a large Bible; but the dim light of the tallow candle which burnt on the table, with its wick of twisted rag, hardly made the corners visible. Beside the table sat a young woman, her head resting on her folded arms, the light of the tallow candle falling full on her head of pale flaxen hair, a little tumbled, and drawn behind into a large knot. The arms crossed on the table, from which the cotton sleeves had fallen back, were the full, rounded arms of one very young.

The older woman, who had just entered, walked to the fireplace, and kneeling down before it took from her apron the twigs and sticks she had gathered and heaped them under the kettle till a blaze sprang up which illumined the whole room. Then she rose up and sat down on a chair before the fire, but facing the table, with her hands crossed on her brown apron.

She was a woman, of fifty, spare and broad-shouldered,

with black hair, already slightly streaked with gray; from below high, arched eyebrows, and a high forehead, full dark eyes looked keenly, and a sharply cut aquiline nose gave strength to the face; but the mouth below was somewhat sensitive, and not over-full. She crossed and recrossed her knotted hands on her brown apron.

The woman at the table moaned and moved her head from side to side. "What time is it?" she asked.

The older woman crossed the room to where the hunting watch hung on the wall.

It showed a quarter-past one, she said, and went back to her seat before the fire, and sat watching the figure beside the table, the firelight bathing her strong upright form and sharp aquiline profile.

Nearly fifty years before, her parents had left the Cape Colony, and had set out on the long trek northward, and she, a young child, had been brought with them. She had no remembrance of the colonial home. Her first dim memories were of traveling in an ox-wagon; of dark nights when a fire was lighted in the open air, and people sat round it on the ground, and some faces seemed to stand out more than others in her memory which she thought must be those of her father and mother and of an old grandmother; she could remember lying awake in the back of the wagon while it was moving on, and the stars were shining down on her; and she had a vague memory of great wide plains with buck on them, which she thought must have been in the Free State. But the first thing which sprang out sharp and clear from the past was a day when she and another child, a little boy cousin of her own age, were playing among the bushes on the bank of a stream;

she remembered how, suddenly, as they looked through the bushes, they saw black men leap out, and mount the ox-wagon outspanned under the trees; she remembered how they shouted and dragged people along, and stabbed them; she remembered how the blood gushed, and how they, the two young children among the bushes, lay flat on their stomachs and did not move or breathe, with that strange self-preserving instinct found in the young of animals or men who grow up in the open.

She remembered how black smoke came out at the back of the wagon and then red tongues of flame through the top; and even that some of the branches of the tree under which the wagon stood caught fire. She remembered later, when the black men had gone, and it was dark, that they were very hungry, and crept out to where the wagon had stood, and that they looked about on the ground for any scraps of food they might pick up, and that when they could not find any they cried. She remembered nothing clearly after that till some men with large beards and large hats rode up on horseback: it might have been next day or the day after. She remembered how they jumped off their horses and took them up in their arms, and how they cried; but that they, the children, did not cry, they only asked for food. She remembered how one man took a bit of thick, cold roaster-cake out of his pocket, and gave it to her, and how nice it tasted. And she remembered that the men took them up before them on their horses, and that one man tied her close to him with a large red handkerchief.

In the years that came she learnt to know that that which she remembered so clearly was the great and ter-

rible day when, at Weenen, and in the country round,
hundreds of women and children and youths and old men
fell before the Zulus, and the assegais of Dingaan's braves
drank blood.

She learnt that on that day all of her house and name,
from the grandmother to the baby in arms, fell, and that
she only and the boy cousin, who had hidden with her
among the bushes, were left of all her kin in that northern
world. She learnt, too, that the man who tied her to him
with the red handkerchief took them back to his wagon,
and that he and his wife adopted them, and brought them
up among their own children.

She remembered, though less clearly than the day of
the fire, how a few years later they trekked away from
Natal, and went through great mountain ranges, ranges
in and near which lay those places the world was to know
later as Laings Nek, and Amajuba, and Ingogo; Elands-
laagte, Nicholson Nek, and Spion Kop. She remembered
how at last after many wanderings they settled down near
the Witwaters Rand where game was plentiful and wild
beasts were dangerous, but there were no natives, and
they were far from the English rule.

There the two children grew up among the children of
those who had adopted them, and were kindly treated by
them as though they were their own; it yet was but natural
that these two of the same name and blood should grow
up with a peculiar tenderness for each other. And so it
came to pass that when they were both eighteen years old
they asked consent of the old people, who gave it gladly,
that they should marry. For a time the young couple lived
on in the house with the old; but after three years they

gathered together all their few goods and in their wagon, with their guns and ammunition and a few sheep and cattle, they moved away northward to found their own home.

For a time they traveled here and traveled there, but at last they settled on a spot where game was plentiful and the soil good, and there among the low undulating slopes, near the bank of a dry sloot, the young man built at last, with his own hands, a little house of two rooms.

On the long slope across the sloot before the house, he plowed a piece of land and enclosed it, and he built kraals for his stock and so struck root in the land and wandered no more. Those were brave, glad, free days to the young couple. They lived largely on the game which the gun brought down, antelope and wildebeest that wandered even past the doors at night; and now and again a lion was killed: one no farther than the door of the round hut behind the house where the meat and the milk were stored, and two were killed at the kraals. Sometimes, too, traders came with their wagons and in exchange for skins and fine horns sold sugar and coffee and print and tan cord, and such things as the little household had need of. The lands yielded richly to them, in maize, and pumpkins, and sweet cane, and melons; and they had nothing to wish for. Then in time three little sons were born to them, who grew as strong and vigorous in the free life of the open veld as the young lions in the long grass and scrub near the river four miles away. Those were joyous, free years for the man and woman, in which disease, and carking care, and anxiety played no part.

Then came a day when their eldest son was ten years

old, and the father went out a-hunting with his Kaffir
servants: in the evening they brought him home with a
wound eight inches long in his side where a lioness had
torn him; they brought back her skin also, as he had shot
her at last in the hand-to-throat struggle. He lingered for
three days and then died. His wife buried him on the low
slope to the left of the house; she and her Kaffir servants
alone made the grave and put him in it, for there were no
white men near. Then she and her sons lived on there; a
new root driven deep into the soil and binding them to it
through the grave on the hillside. She hung her husband's
large hunting watch up on the wall, and put three of his
guns over it on the rack, and the gun he had in his hand
when he met his death she took down and polished up
every day; but one gun she always kept loaded at the head
of her bed in the inner room. She counted the stock every
night and saw that the Kaffirs plowed the lands, and she
saw to the planting and watering of them herself.

Often as the years passed, men of the countryside, and
even from far off, heard of the young handsome widow
who lived alone with her children and saw to her own
stock and lands; and they came a-courting. But many of
them were afraid to say anything when once they had
come, and those who had spoken to her, when once she
had answered them, never came again. About this time
too the countryside began to fill in; and people came
and settled as near as eight and ten miles away; and as
people increased, the game began to vanish, and with the
game the lions, so that the one her husband killed was
almost the last ever seen there. But there was still game
enough for food, and when her eldest son was twelve years

old, and she gave him his father's smallest gun to go out hunting with, he returned home almost every day with meat enough for the household tied behind his saddle. And as time passed she came also to be known through the countryside as a "wise woman." People came to her to ask advice about their illnesses, or to ask her to dress old wounds that would not heal; and when they questioned her whether she thought the rains would be early, or the game plentiful that year, she was nearly always right. So they called her a "wise woman" because neither she nor they knew any word in that up-country speech of theirs for the thing called "genius." So all things went well till the eldest son was eighteen, and the dark beard was beginning to sprout on his face, and his mother began to think that soon there might be a daughter in the house; for on Saturday evenings, when his work was done, he put on his best clothes and rode off to the next farm eight miles away, where was a young daughter. His mother always saw that he had a freshly ironed shirt waiting for him on his bed, when he came home from the kraals on Saturday nights, and she made plans as to how they would build on two rooms for the new daughter. At this time he was training young horses to have them ready to sell when the traders came round: he was a fine rider and it was always his work. One afternoon he mounted a young horse before the door and it bucked and threw him. He had often fallen before, but this time his neck was broken. He lay dead with his head two feet from his mother's doorstep. They took up his tall, strong body and the next day the neighbors came from the next farm and they buried him beside his father, on the hillside, and another root was struck into the soil.

Then the three who were left in the little farmhouse lived and worked on as before, for a year and more.

Then a small native war broke out, and the young burghers of the district were called out to help. The second son was very young, but he was the best shot in the district, so he went away with the others. Three months after, the men came back, but among the few who did not return was her son. On a hot sunny afternoon, walking through a mealie field which they thought was deserted and where the dried yellow stalks stood thick, an assegai thrown from an unseen hand found him, and he fell there. His comrades took him and buried him under a large thorn tree, and scraped the earth smooth over him, that his grave might not be found by others. So he was not laid on the rise to the left of the house with his kindred, but his mother's heart went often to that thorn tree in the far north.

And now again there were only two in the little mudhouse, as there had been years before when the young man and wife first settled there. She and her young lad were always together night and day, and did all that they did together, as though they were mother and daughter. He was a fair lad, tall and gentle as his father had been before him, not huge and dark as his two elder brothers; but he seemed to ripen toward manhood early. When he was only sixteen the thick white down was already gathering heavy on his upper lip; his mother watched him narrowly, and had many thoughts in her heart. One evening as they sat twisting wicks for the candles together, she said to him, "You will be eighteen on your next birthday, my son; that was your father's age when he married me." He

said, "Yes," and they spoke no more then. But later in the
evening when they sat before the door she said to him,
"We are very lonely here. I often long to hear the feet of
a little child about the house and to see one with your
father's blood in it play before the door as you and your
brothers played. Have you ever thought that you are the
last of your father's name and blood left here in the north,
that if you died there would be none left?" He said he had
thought of it. Then she told him she thought it would be
well if he went away, to the part of the country where
the people lived who had brought her up: several of the
sons and daughters who had grown up with her had now
grown-up children. He might go down and from among
them seek out a young girl whom he liked and who liked
him; and if he found her, bring her back as a wife. The lad
thought very well of his mother's plan. And when three
months were passed, and the plowing season was over, he
rode away one day, on the best black horse they had, his
Kaffir boy riding behind him on another, and his mother
stood at the gable watching them ride away. For three
months she heard nothing of him, for trains were not in
those days, and letters came rarely and by chance, and
neither he nor she could read or write. One afternoon she
stood at the gable end as she always stood when her work
was done, looking out along the road that came over the
rise, and she saw a large tent-wagon coming along it, and
her son walking beside it. She walked to meet it. When
she had greeted her son and climbed into the wagon she
found there a girl of fifteen with pale flaxen hair and large
blue eyes whom he had brought home as his wife. Her
father had given her the wagon and oxen as her wedding

portion. The older woman's heart wrapt itself about the girl as though she had been the daughter she had dreamed to bear of her own body, and had never borne.

The three lived joyfully at the little house as though they were one person. The young wife had been accustomed to live in a larger house, and down south, where they had things they had not here. She had been to school, and learned to read and write, and she could even talk a little English; but she longed for none of the things which she had had; the little brown house was home enough for her.

After a year a child came, but, whether it were that the mother was too young, it only opened its eyes for an hour on the world and closed them again. The young mother wept bitterly, but her husband folded his arms about her, and the mother comforted both. "You are young, my children, but we shall yet hear the sound of children's voices in the house," she said; and after a little while the young mother was well again and things went on peacefully as before in the little home.

But in the land things were not going on peacefully. That was the time that the flag to escape from—which the people had left their old homes in the Colony, and had again left Natal when it followed them there, and had chosen to face the spear of the savage, and the conflict with wild beasts, and death by hunger and thirst in the wilderness rather than live under—had by force and fraud unfurled itself over them again. For the moment a great sullen silence brooded over the land. The people, slow of thought, slow of speech, determined in action, and unforgetting, sat still and waited. It was like the silence that rests over the land before an up-country thunderstorm breaks.

Then words came, "They have not even given us the free government they promised"—then acts—the people rose. Even in that remote countryside the men began to mount their horses, and with their guns ride away to help. In the little mud-house the young wife wept much when he said that he too was going. But when his mother helped him pack his saddle bags she helped too, and on the day when the men from the next farm went, he rode away also with his gun by his side.

No direct news of the one they had sent away came to the waiting women at the farmhouse; then came fleet reports of the victories of Ingogo and Amajuba. Then came an afternoon after he had been gone two months. They had both been to the gable end to look out at the road, as they did continually amid their work, and they had just come in to drink their afternoon coffee when the Kaffir maid ran in to say she saw someone coming along the road who looked like her master. The women ran out. It was the white horse on which he had ridden away, but they almost doubted if it were he. He rode bending on his saddle, with his chin on his breast and his arm hanging at his side. At first they thought he had been wounded, but when they had helped him from his horse and brought him into the house they found it was only a deadly fever which was upon him. He had crept home to them by small stages. Hardly had he any spirit left to tell them of Ingogo, Laings Nek, and Amajuba. For fourteen days he grew worse and on the fifteenth day he died. And the two women buried him where the rest of his kin lay on the hillside.

And so it came to pass that on that warm starlight night

the two women were alone in the little mud-house with the stillness of the veld about them; even their Kaffir servants asleep in their huts beyond the kraals; and the very sheep lying silent in the starlight. They two were alone in the little house, but they knew that before morning they would not be alone, they were awaiting the coming of the dead man's child.

The young woman with her head on the table groaned. "If only my husband were here still," she wailed. The old woman rose and stood beside her, passing her hard, work-worn hand gently over her shoulder as if she were a little child. At last she induced her to go and lie down in the inner room. When she had grown quieter and seemed to have fallen into a light sleep the old woman came to the front room again. It was almost two o'clock and the fire had burned low under the large kettle. She scraped the coals together and went out of the front door to fetch more wood, and closed the door behind her. The night air struck cool and fresh upon her face after the close air of the house; the stars seemed to be growing lighter as the night advanced, they shot down their light as from a million polished steel points. She walked to the back of the house where, beyond the round hut that served as a storeroom, the woodpile lay. She bent down gathering sticks and chips till her apron was full, then slowly she raised herself and stood still. She looked upward. It was a wonderful night. The white band of the Milky Way crossed the sky overhead, and from every side, stars threw down their light, sharp as barbed spears, from the velvety blue-black of the sky. The woman raised her hand to her forehead as if pushing the hair farther off it, and stood motionless, looking up. After a long time she dropped her hand and began walking slowly toward the house. Yet once or twice on the way she paused and stood looking up. When she went into the house the woman in the inner room was again moving and moaning. She laid the sticks down before the fire and went into the next room. She bent down over the bed where the younger woman lay, and put her hand upon her. "My daughter," she said slowly, "be comforted. A wonderful thing has happened to me. As I stood out in the starlight it was as though a voice came down to me and spoke. The child which will be born of you tonight will be a man-child, and he will live to do great things for his land and for his people."

Before morning there was the sound of a little wail in the mud-house: and the child who was to do great things for his land and for his people was born.

II

Six years passed; and all was as it had been at the little house among the slopes. Only a new piece of land had been plowed up and added to the land before the house, so that the plowed land now almost reached to the ridge.

The young mother had grown stouter, and lost her pink and white; she had become a working woman, but she still had the large knot of flaxen hair behind her head and the large wondering eyes. She had many suitors in those six years, but she sent them all away. She said the old woman looked after the farm as well as any man might, and her son would be grown up by and by. The grandmother's hair was a little more streaked with gray, but it was as thick as ever, and her shoulders as upright; only some of her front teeth had fallen out, which made her lips close more softly.

The great change was that wherever the women went there was the flaxen-haired child to walk beside them holding on to their skirts or clasping their hands.

The neighbors said they were ruining the child: they let his hair grow long, like a girl's, because it curled; and they never let him wear veldschoens like other children but always shop boots; and his mother sat up at night to iron his pinafores as if the next day were always a Sunday.

But the women cared nothing for what was said; to them he was not as any other child. He asked them strange questions they could not answer, and he never troubled them by wishing to go and play with the little Kaffirs as other children trouble. When neighbors came over and brought their children with them he ran away and hid in the sloot to play by himself till they were gone. No, he was not like other children!

When the women went to lie down on hot days after dinner sometimes, he would say that he did not want to sleep; but he would not run about and make a noise like other children—he would go and sit outside in the shade of the house, on the front doorstep, quite still, with his little hands resting on his knees, and stare far away at the plowed lands on the slope, or the shadows nearer; the women would open the bedroom window, and peep out to look at him as he sat there.

The child loved his mother and followed her about to the milk house, and to the kraals; but he loved his grandmother best.

She told him stories.

When she went to the lands to see how the Kaffirs were plowing he would run at her side holding her dress; when they had gone a short way he would tug gently at it and say, "Grandmother, tell me things!"

And long before day broke, when it was yet quite dark, he would often creep from the bed where he slept with his mother into his grandmother's bed in the corner; he would put his arms round her neck and stroke her face till she woke, and then whisper softly, "Tell me stories!" and she would tell them to him in a low voice not to wake the mother, till the cock crowed and it was time to get up and light the candle and the fire.

But what he liked best of all were the hot, still summer nights, when the women put their chairs before the door because it was too warm to go to sleep; and he would sit on the stool at his grandmother's feet and lean his head against her knees, and she would tell him on and on of the things he liked to hear; and he would watch the stars as they slowly set along the ridge, or the moonlight, casting bright-edged shadows from the gable as she talked. Often after the mother had got sleepy and gone in to bed the two sat there together.

The stories she told him were always true stories of the things she had seen or of things she had heard. Sometimes they were stories of her own childhood: of the day when she and his grandfather hid among the bushes, and saw the wagon burnt; sometimes they were of the long trek from Natal to the Transvaal; sometimes of the things which happened to her and his grandfather when first they came to that spot among the ridges, of how there was no house there nor lands, only two bare grassy slopes when they outspanned their wagon there the first night; she told of a lion she once found when she opened the door in the morning, sitting, with paws crossed, upon the threshold, and how the grandfather jumped out of bed and re-opened the door two inches, and shot it through the opening; the skin was kept in the round storehouse still, very old and mangy.

Sometimes she told him of the two uncles who were dead, and of his own father, and of all they had been and done. But sometimes she told him of things much farther off: of the old Colony where she had been born, but which she could not remember, and of the things which happened there in the old days. She told him of how the British had taken the Cape over, and of how the English had hanged their men at the "Slachters Nek" for resisting the English government, and of how the friends and relations had been made to stand round to see them hanged whether they would or no, and of how the scaffold broke down as they were being hanged, and the people looking on cried aloud, "It is the finger of God! They are saved!" but how the British hanged them up again. She told him of the great trek in which her parents had taken part to escape from under the British flag; of the great battles with Moselikatse; and of the murder of Retief and his men by Dingaan, and of Dingaan's Day. She told him how the British government followed them into Natal, and of how they trekked north and east to escape from it again; and she told him of the later things, of the fight at Laings Nek, and Ingogo, and Amajuba, where his father had been. Always she told the same story in exactly the same words over and over again, till the child knew them all by heart, and would ask for this and then that.

The story he loved best, and asked for more often than all the others, made his grandmother wonder, because it did not seem to her the story a child would best like; it was not a story of lion-hunting, or wars, or adventures. Continually when she asked what she should tell him, he said, "About the mountains!"

It was the story of how the Boer women in Natal when the English Commissioner came to annex their country, collected to meet him and pointing toward the Drakens Berg Mountains said, "We go across those mountains to freedom or to death!"

More than once, when she was telling him the story, she saw him stretch out his little arm and raise his hand, as though he were speaking.

One evening as he and his mother were coming home from the milking kraals, and it was getting dark, and he was very tired, having romped about shouting among the young calves and kids all the evening, he held her hand tightly.

"Mother," he said suddenly, "when I am grown up, I am going to Natal." "Why, my child?" she asked him; "there are none of our family living there now."

He waited a little, then said, very slowly, "I am going to go and try to get our land back!"

His mother started; if there were one thing she was more firmly resolved on in her own mind than any other it was that he should never go to the wars. She began to talk quickly of the old white cow who had kicked the pail over as she was milked, and when she got to the house she did not even mention to the grandmother what had happened; it seemed better to forget.

One night in the rainy season when it was damp and chilly they sat round the large fireplace in the front room.

Outside the rain was pouring in torrents and you could hear the water rushing in the great dry sloot before the door. His grandmother, to amuse him, had sprung some dried mealies in the great black pot and sprinkled them with sugar, and now he sat on the stool at her feet with a large lump of the sticky sweetmeat in his hand, watching the fire. His grandmother from above him was watching it also, and his mother in her elbow-chair on the other side of the fire had her eyes half closed and was nodding already with the warmth of the room and her long day's work. The child sat so quiet, the hand with the lump of sweetmeat resting on his knee, that his grandmother thought he had gone to sleep too. Suddenly he said without looking up, "Grandmother?"

"Yes."

He waited rather a long time, then said slowly, "Grandmother, did God make the English too?"

She also waited for a while, then she said, "Yes, my child; He made all things."

They were silent again, and there was no sound but of the rain falling and the fire cracking and the sloot rushing outside. Then he threw his head backward on to his grandmother's knee and looking up into her face, said, "But, grandmother, why did He make them?"

Then she too was silent for a long time. "My child," at last she said, "we cannot judge the ways of the Almighty. He does that which seems good in His own eyes."

The child sat up and looked back at the fire. Slowly he tapped his knee with the lump of sweetmeat once or twice; then he began to munch it; and soon the mother started wide awake and said it was time for all to go to bed.

The next morning his grandmother sat on the front doorstep cutting beans in an iron basin; he sat beside her on the step pretending to cut too, with a short, broken knife. Presently he left off and rested his hands on his knees, looking away at the hedge beyond, with his small forehead knit tight between the eyes.

"Grandmother," he said suddenly, in a small, almost shrill voice, "do the English want *all* the lands of *all* the people?"

The handle of his grandmother's knife as she cut clinked against the iron side of the basin. "All they can get," she said.

After a while he made a little movement almost like a sigh, and took up his little knife again and went on cutting.

Some time after that, when a trader came by, his grandmother bought him a spelling book and a slate and pencils, and his mother began to teach him to read and write. When she had taught him for a year he knew all she did. Sometimes when she was setting him a copy and left a letter out in a word, he would quietly take the pencil when she set it down and put the letter in, not with any idea of correcting her, but simply because it must be there.

Often at night when the child had gone to bed early, tired out with his long day's play, and the two women were left in the front room with the tallow candle burning on the table between them, then they talked of his future.

Ever since he had been born everything they had earned had been put away in the wagon chest under the grandmother's bed. When the traders with their wagons came round, the women bought nothing except a few groceries and clothes for the child; even before they bought a yard of cotton print for a new apron they talked long and solemnly as to whether the old one might not be made to do by repatching; and they mixed much more dry pumpkin and corn with their coffee than before he was born. It was to earn more money that the large new piece of land had been added to the lands before the house.

They were going to have him educated. First he was to be taught all they could at home, then to be sent away to a great school in the old Colony, and then he was to go over the sea to Europe and come back an advocate or a doctor or a parson. The grandmother had made a long journey to the next town to find out from the minister just how much it would cost to do it all.

In the evenings when they sat talking it over, the mother generally inclined to his becoming a parson. She never told the grandmother why, but the real reason was because parsons do not go to the wars. The grandmother generally favored his becoming an advocate, because he might become judge. Sometimes they sat discussing these matters till the candle almost burnt out.

"Perhaps, one day," the mother would at last say, "he may yet become President!"

Then the grandmother would slowly refold her hands across her apron and say softly, "Who knows?—who knows?"

Often they would get the box out from under the bed (looking carefully across to the corner to see he was fast asleep) and would count out all the money, though each knew to a farthing how much was there; then they would make it into little heaps, so much for this, so much for that, and then they would count on their fingers how many good seasons it would take to make the rest, and how old he would be.

When he was eight and had learnt all his mother could teach him, they sent him to school every day on an adjoining farm six miles off, where the people had a schoolmaster. Every day he rode over on the great white horse his father went to the wars with; his mother was afraid to let him ride alone at first, but his grandmother said he must learn to do everything alone. At four o'clock when he came back one or other of the women was always looking out to see the little figure on the tall horse coming over the ridge.

When he was eleven they gave him his father's smallest gun; and one day not long after, he came back with his first small buck. His mother had the skin dressed and bound with red, and she laid it as a mat under the table, and even the horns she did not throw away, and saved them in the round house, because it was his first.

When he was fourteen the schoolmaster said he could teach him no more; that he ought to go to some larger school where they taught Latin and other difficult things; they had not yet money enough and he was not quite old enough to go to the old Colony, so they sent him first to the Highveld, where his mother's relations lived and where there were good schools, where they taught the difficult things; he could live with his mother's relations and come back once a year for the holidays.

They were great times when he came.

His mother made him koekies and sasarties and nice things every day; and he used to sit on the stool at her feet and let her play with his hair like when he was quite small. With his grandmother he talked. He tried to explain to her all he was learning; and he read the English newspapers to her (she could neither read in English nor Dutch), translating them. Most of all she liked his atlas. They would sometimes sit over it for half an hour in the evening tracing the different lands and talking of them. On the warm nights he used still to sit outside on the stool at her feet with his head against her knee, and they used to discuss things that were happening in other lands and in South Africa; and sometimes they sat there quite still together.

It was now he who had the most stories to tell; he had seen Krugersdorp, and Johannesburg, and Pretoria; he knew the world; he was at Krugersdorp when Dr. Jameson made his raid. Sometimes he sat for an hour, telling her of things, and she sat quietly listening.

When he was seventeen, nearly eighteen, there was money enough in the box to pay for his going to the Colony and then to Europe; and he came home to spend a few months with them before he went.

He was very handsome now; not tall, and very slight, but with fair hair that curled close to his head, and white hands like a townsman. All the girls in the countryside were in love with him. They all wished he would come and see them. But he seldom rode from home except to go to the next farm where he had been at school. There lived little Aletta, who was the daughter of the woman his uncle had loved before he went to the Kaffir war and got killed. She was only fifteen years old, but they had always been great friends. She netted him a purse of green silk. He said he would take it with him to Europe, and would show it to her when he came back and was an advocate; and he gave her a book with her name written in it, which she was to show to him.

These were the days when the land was full of talk; it was said the English were landing troops in South Africa, and wanted to have war. Often the neighbors from the nearest farms would come to talk about it (there were more farms now, the country was filling in, and the nearest railway station was only a day's journey off), and they discussed matters. Some said they thought there would be war; others again laughed, and said it would be only Jameson and his white flag again. But the grandmother shook her head, and if they asked her, "Why," she said, "it will not be the war of a week, nor of a month; if it comes it will be the war of years," but she would say nothing more.

Yet sometimes when she and her grandson were walking along together in the lands she would talk.

Once she said, "It is as if a great heavy cloud hung just above my head, as though I wished to press it back with my hands and could not. It will be a great war—a great war. Perhaps the English government will take the land for a time, but they will not keep it. The gold they have fought for will divide them, till they slay one another over it."

Another day she said, "This land will be a great land one day with one people from the sea to the north—but we shall not live to see it."

He said to her, "But how can that be when we are all of different races?"

She said, "The land will make us one. Were not our fathers of more than one race?"

Another day, when she and he were sitting by the table after dinner, she pointed to a sheet of exercise paper, on which he had been working out a problem and which was covered with algebraic symbols, and said, "In fifteen years' time the government of England will not have one piece of land in all South Africa as large as that sheet of paper."

One night when the milking had been late and she and he were walking down together from the kraals in the starlight she said to him, "If this war comes, let no man go to it lightly, thinking he will surely return home, nor let him go expecting victory on the next day. It will come at last, but not at first."

"Sometimes," she said, "I wake at night and it is as though the whole house were filled with smoke—and I have to get up and go outside to breathe. It is as though I saw my whole land blackened and desolate. But when I look up it is as though a voice cried out to me, 'Have no fear!'"

They were getting his things ready for him to go away after Christmas. His mother was making him shirts and his grandmother was having a kaross of jackals' skins made that he might take it with him to Europe where it was so cold. But his mother noticed that whenever the grandmother was in the room with him and he was not looking at her, her eyes were always curiously fixed on him as though they were questioning something. The hair was growing white and a little thin over her temples now, but her eyes were as bright as ever, and she could do a day's work with any man.

One day when the youth was at the kraals helping the Kaffir boys to mend a wall, and the mother was kneading bread in the front room, and the grandmother washing up the breakfast things, the son of the Field Cornet came riding over from his father's farm, which was about twelve miles off. He stopped at the kraal and Jan and he stood talking for some time, then they walked down to the farmhouse, the Kaffir boy leading the horse behind them. Jan stopped at the round store, but the Field Cornet's son went to the front door. The grandmother asked him in, and handed him some coffee, and the mother, her hands still in the dough, asked him how things were going at his father's farm, and if his mother's young turkeys had come out well, and she asked if he had met Jan at the kraals. He answered the questions slowly and sipped his coffee. Then he put the cup down on the table and said suddenly in the same measured voice, staring at the wall in front of him, that war had broken out, and his father had sent him round to call out all fighting burghers.

The mother took her hands out of the dough and stood upright beside the trough as though paralyzed. Then she cried in a high, hard voice, unlike her own, "Yes, but Jan cannot go! He is hardly eighteen! He's got to go and be educated in other lands! You can't take the only son of a widow!"

"Aunt," said the young man slowly, "no one will make him go."

The grandmother stood resting the knuckles of both

hands on the table, her eyes fixed on the young man. "He shall decide himself," she said.

The mother wiped her hands from the dough and rushed past them and out the door; the grandmother followed slowly.

They found him in the shade at the back of the house, sitting on a stump; he was cleaning the belt of his new Mauser which lay across his knees.

"Jan," his mother cried, grasping his shoulder, "you are not going away? You can't go! You must stay. You can go by Delagoa Bay if there is fighting on the other side! There is plenty of money!"

He looked softly up into her face with his blue eyes. "We have all to be at the Field Cornet's at nine o'clock tomorrow morning," he said. She wept aloud and argued.

His grandmother turned slowly without speaking, and went back into the house. When she had given the Field Cornet's son another cup of coffee, and shaken hands with him, she went into the bedroom and opened the box in which her grandson's clothes were kept, to see which things he should take with him. After a time the mother came back too. He had kissed her and talked to her until she too had at last said it was right he should go.

All day they were busy. His mother baked him biscuits to take in his bag, and his grandmother made a belt of two strips of leather; she sewed them together herself and put a few sovereigns between the stitchings. She said some of his comrades might need the money if he did not.

The next morning early he was ready. There were two saddlebags tied to his saddle and before it was strapped the kaross his grandmother had made; she said it would be useful when he had to sleep on damp ground. When he had greeted them, he rode away toward the rise: and the women stood at the gable of the house to watch him.

When he had gone a little way he turned in his saddle, and they could see he was smiling; he took off his hat and waved it in the air; the early morning sunshine made his hair as yellow as the tassels that hang from the head of ripening mealies. His mother covered her face with the sides of her kappie and wept aloud; but the grandmother shaded her eyes with both her hands and stood watching him till the figure passed out of sight over the ridge; and when it was gone and the mother returned to the house crying, she still stood watching the line against the sky.

The two women were very quiet during the next days; they worked hard, and seldom spoke. After eight days there came a long letter from him (there was now a post once a week from the station to the Field Cornet's). He said he was well and in very good spirits. He had been to Krugersdorp, and Johannesburg, and Pretoria; all the family living there were well and sent greetings. He had joined a corps that was leaving for the front the next day. He sent also a long message to Aletta, asking them to tell her he was sorry to go away without saying goodbye; and he told his mother how good the biscuits and biltong were she had put into his saddlebag; and he sent her a piece of "vierkleur" ribbon in the letter, to wear on her breast.

The women talked a great deal for a day or two after this letter came. Eight days after, there was a short note from him, written in pencil in the train on his way to the front. He said all was going well, and if he did not write soon they were not to be anxious; he would write as often as he could.

For some days the women discussed the note too.

Then came two weeks without a letter; the two women became very silent. Every day, they sent the Kaffir boy over to the Field Cornet's, even on the days when there was no post, to hear if there was any news.

Many reports were flying about the countryside. Some said that an English armored train had been taken on the western border; that there had been fighting at Albertina, and in Natal. But nothing seemed quite certain.

Another week passed. . . . Then the two women became very quiet.

The grandmother, when she saw her daughter-in-law left the food untouched on her plate, said there was no need to be anxious; men at the front could not always find paper and pencils to write with and might be far from any post office. Yet night after night she herself would rise from her bed saying she felt the house close, and go and walk up and down outside.

Then one day suddenly all their servants left them except one Kaffir and his wife, whom they had had for years, and the servants from the farms about went also, which was a sign there had been news of much fighting; for the Kaffirs hear things long before the white man knows them.

Three days after, as the women were clearing off the breakfast things, the youngest son of the Field Cornet, who was only fifteen and had not gone to the war with the others, rode up. He hitched his horse to the post, and came toward the door. The mother stepped forward to meet him and shook hands in the doorway.

"I suppose you have come for the carrot seed I promised your mother? I was not able to send it, as our servants ran away," she said, as she shook his hand. "There isn't a letter from Jan, is there?" The lad said no, there was no letter from him, and shook hands with the grandmother. He stood by the table instead of sitting down.

The mother turned to the fireplace to get coals to put under the coffee to rewarm it; but the grandmother stood leaning forward with her eyes fixed on him from across the table. He felt uneasily in his breast pocket.

"Is there no news?" the mother said without looking round, as she bent over the fire.

"Yes, there is news, Aunt."

She rose quickly and turned toward him, putting down the brazier on the table. He took a letter out of his breast pocket. "Aunt, my father said I must bring this to you. It came inside one to him and they asked him to send one of us over with it."

The mother took the letter; she held it, examining the address.

"It looks to me like the writing of Sister Annie's Paul," she said. "Perhaps there is news of Jan in it"—she turned to them with a half-nervous smile—"they were always such friends."

"All is as God wills, Aunt," the young man said, looking down fixedly at the top of his riding whip.

But the grandmother leaned forward motionless, watching her daughter-in-law as she opened the letter.

She began to read to herself, her lips moving slowly as she deciphered it word by word.

Then a piercing cry rang through the roof of the little mud farmhouse. "He is dead! My boy is dead!"

She flung the letter on the table and ran out the front door.

Far out across the quiet plowed lands and over the veld to where the kraals lay the cry rang. The Kaffir woman who sat outside her hut beyond the kraals nursing her baby heard it and came down with her child across her hip to see what was the matter. At the side of the round house she stood motionless and open-mouthed, watching the woman, who paced up and down behind the house with her apron thrown over her head and her hands folded above it, crying aloud.

In the front room the grandmother, who had not spoken since he came, took up the letter and put it in the lad's hands. "Read," she whispered. And slowly the lad spelled it out.

My Dear Aunt,

I hope this letter finds you well. The Commandant has asked me to write it.

We had a great fight four days ago, and Jan is dead. The Commandant says I must tell you how it happened. Aunt, there were five of us first in a position on that koppie, but two got killed, and then there were only three of us— Jan, and I, and Uncle Peter's Frikkie. Aunt, the khakies were coming on all round just like locusts, and the bullets were coming just like hail. It was bare on that side of the koppie where we were, but we had plenty of cartridges. We three took up a position where there were some small stones and we fought, Aunt; we had to. One bullet took off the top of my ear, and Jan got two bullets, one through the flesh in the left leg and one through his arm, but he could still fire his gun. Then we three meant to go to the top of the koppie, but a bullet took Jan right through his chest. We knew he couldn't go any farther. The khakis were right at the foot of the koppie just coming up. He told us to lay him down, Aunt. We said we would stay by him, but he said we must go. I put my jacket under his head and Frikkie put his over his feet. We threw his gun far away from him that they might see how it was with him. He said he hadn't much pain, Aunt. He was full of blood from his arm, but there wasn't much from his chest, only a little out of the corners of his mouth. He said we must make haste or the khakies would catch us; he said he wasn't afraid to be left there.

Aunt, when we got to the top, it was all full of khakies like the sea on the other side, all among the koppies and on our koppie too. We were surrounded, Aunt; the last I saw of Frikkie he was sitting on a stone with the blood running down his face, but he got under a rock and hid there; some of our men found him next morning and brought him to camp. Aunt, there was a khakie's horse standing just below where I was, with no one on it. I jumped on and rode. The bullets went this way and the bullets went that, but I rode! Aunt, the khakies were sometimes as near me as that tentpole, only the Grace of God saved me. It was dark in the night when I got back to where our people were, because I had to go round all the koppies to get away from the khakies.

Aunt, the next day we went to look for him. We found

him where we left him; but he was turned over on to his face; they had taken all his things, his belt and his watch, and the puggaree from his hat, even his boots. The little green silk purse he used to carry we found on the ground by him, but nothing in it. I will send it back to you whenever I get an opportunity.

Aunt, when we turned him over on his back there were four bayonet stabs in his body. The doctor says it was only the first three while he was alive; the last one was through his heart and killed him at once.

We gave him a Christian burial, Aunt; we took him to the camp.

The Commandant was there, and all of the family who are with the Commando were there, and they all said they hoped God would comfort you . . .

The old woman leaned forward and grasped the boy's arm. "Read it over again," she said, "from where they found him." He turned back and re-read slowly. She gazed at the page as though she were reading also. Then, suddenly, she slipped out the front door.

At the back of the house she found her daughter-in-law still walking up and down, and the Kaffir woman with a red handkerchief bound round her head and the child sitting across her hip, sucking from her long, pendulous breast, looking on.

The old woman walked up to her daughter-in-law and grasped her firmly by the arm.

"He's dead! You know, my boy's dead!" she cried, drawing the apron down with her right hand and disclosing her swollen and bleared face. "Oh, his beautiful hair— Oh, his beautiful hair!"

The old woman held her arm tighter with both hands; the younger opened her half-closed eyes, and looked into the keen, clear eyes fixed on hers, and stood arrested.

The old woman drew her face closer to hers. "You . . . do . . . not . . . know . . . what . . . has . . . happened!" She spoke slowly, her tongue striking her front gum, the jaw moving stiffly, as though partly paralyzed. She loosed her left hand and held up the curved work-worn fingers before her daughter-in-law's face. "Was it not told me . . . the night he was born . . . here . . . at this spot . . . that he would do great things . . . great things . . . for his land and his people?" She bent forward till her lips almost touched the other's. "Three . . . bullet . . . wounds . . . and four . . . bayonet . . . stabs!" She raised her left hand high in the air. "Three . . . bullet . . . wounds . . . and four . . . bayonet . . . stabs! . . . Is it given to many to die so for their land and their people!"

The younger woman gazed into her eyes, her own growing larger and larger. She let the old woman lead her by the arm in silence into the house.

The Field Cornet's son was gone, feeling there was nothing more to be done; and the Kaffir woman went back with her baby to her hut beyond the kraals. All day the house was very silent. The Kaffir woman wondered that no smoke rose from the farmhouse chimney, and that she was not called to churn, or wash the pots. At three o'clock she went down to the house. As she passed the grated window of the round outhouse she saw the buckets of milk still standing unsifted on the floor as they had been set down at breakfast time, and under the great soap pot beside the wood pile the fire had died out. She went round to the front of the house and saw the door and window shutters still closed, as though her mistresses were still sleeping. So she rebuilt the fire under the soap pot and went back to her hut.

It was four o'clock when the grandmother came out from the dark inner room where she and her daughter-in-law had been lying down; she opened the top of the front door, and lit the fire with twigs, and set the large black kettle over it. When it boiled she made coffee, and poured out two cups and set them on the table with a plate of biscuits, and then called her daughter-in-law from the inner room.

The two women sat down one on each side of the table, with their coffee cups before them, and the biscuits between them, but for a time they said nothing, but sat silent, looking out through the open door at the shadow of the house and the afternoon sunshine beyond it. At last the older woman motioned that the younger should drink her coffee. She took a little, and then folding her arms on the table rested her head on them, and sat motionless as if asleep.

The older woman broke up a biscuit into her own cup, and stirred it round and round; and then, without tasting, sat gazing out into the afternoon's sunshine till it grew cold beside her.

It was five, and the heat was quickly dying; the glorious golden coloring of the later afternoon was creeping over everything when she rose from her chair. She moved to the door and took from behind it two large white calico bags hanging there, and from nails on the wall she took down two large brown cotton kappies. She walked round the table and laid her hand gently on her daughter-in-law's arm. The younger woman raised her head slowly and looked up into her mother-in-law's face; and then, suddenly, she knew that her mother-in-law was an old, old woman. The little shriveled face that looked down at her was hardly larger than a child's; the eyelids were half closed and the lips worked at the corners and the bones cut out through the skin in the temples.

"I am going out to sow—the ground will be getting too dry tomorrow; will you come with me?" she said gently.

The younger woman made a movement with her hand, as though she said, "What is the use?" and redropped her hand on the table.

"It may go on for long; our burghers must have food," the old woman said gently.

The younger woman looked into her face, then she rose slowly and taking one of the brown kappies from her hand, put it on, and hung one of the bags over her left arm; the old woman did the same and together they passed out of the door. As the older woman stepped down, the younger caught her and saved her from falling.

"Take my arm, mother," she said.

But the old woman drew her shoulders up. "I only stumbled a little!" she said quickly. "That step has been always too high." But before she reached the plank over the sloot, the shoulders had drooped again, and the neck fallen forward.

The mold in the lands was black and soft; it lay in long ridges, as it had been plowed up a week before, but the last night's rain had softened it and made it moist and ready for putting in the seed.

The bags which the women carried on their arms were full of the seed of pumpkins and mealies. They began to walk up the lands, keeping parallel with the low hedge of dried bushes that ran up along the side of the sloot almost up to the top of the ridge. At every few paces they stopped and bent down to press into the earth, now one and then the other kind of seed from their bags. Slowly they walked up and down till they reached the top of the land almost on the horizon line; and then they turned, and walked down, sowing as they went. When they had reached the bottom of the land before the farmhouse it was almost sunset, and their bags were nearly empty; but they turned to go up once more. The light of the setting sun cast long, gaunt shadows from their figures across the plowed land, over the low hedge and the sloot, into the bare veld beyond; shadows that grew longer and longer as they passed slowly on, pressing in the seeds . . . The seeds! . . . that were to lie in the dank, dark, earth, and rot there, seemingly, to die, till their outer covering had split and fallen from them . . . and then, when the rains had fallen, and the sun had shone, to come up above the earth again, and high in the clear air to lift their feathery plumes and hang out their pointed leaves and silken tassels! To cover the ground with a mantle of green and gold through which sunlight quivered, over which the insects hung by thousands, carrying yellow pollen on their legs and wings and making the air alive with their hum and stir, while grain and fruit ripened surely . . . for the next season's harvest!

When the sun had set, the two women with their empty bags turned and walked silently home in the dark to the farmhouse.

NINETEEN HUNDRED AND ONE

Near one of the camps in the Northern Transvaal are the graves of two women. The older one died first, on the twenty-third of the month, from hunger and want; the younger woman tended her with ceaseless care and devotion till the end. A week later when the British superintendent came round to inspect the tents, she was found lying on her blanket on the mud floor dead, with the rations of bread and meat she had got four days before untouched on a box beside her. Whether she died of disease, or from inability to eat the food, no one could say. Some who had seen her said she hardly seemed to care to live after the old woman died; they buried them side by side. There is no stone and no name upon either grave to say who lies there . . . our unknown . . . our unnamed . . . our forgotten dead.

IN THE YEAR NINETEEN HUNDRED AND FOUR

If you look for the little farmhouse among the ridges you will not find it there today.

The English soldiers burnt it down. You can only see where the farmhouse once stood, because the stramonia and weeds grow high and very strong there; and where the plowed lands were you can only tell, because the veld never grows quite the same on land that has once been plowed. Only a brown patch among the long grass on the ridge shows where the kraals and huts once were.

In a country house in the north of England the owner has upon his wall an old flintlock gun. He takes it down to show his friends. It is a small thing he picked up in the war in South Africa, he says. It must be at least eighty years old and is very valuable. He shows how curiously it is constructed; he says it must have been kept in such perfect repair by continual polishing for the steel shines as if it were silver. He does not tell that he took it from the wall of the little mud house before he burnt it down.

It was the grandfather's gun, which the women had kept polished on the wall.

In a London drawing room the descendant of a long line of titled forefathers entertains her guests. It is a fair room, and all that money can buy to make life soft and beautiful is there.

On the carpet stands a little dark wooden stool. When one of her guests notices it, she says it is a small curiosity which her son brought home to her from South Africa when he was out in the war there; and how good it was of him to think of her when he was away in the back country. And when they ask what it is, she says it is a thing Boer women have as a footstool and to keep their feet warm; and she shows the hole at the side where they put the coals in, and the little holes at the top where the heat comes out.

And the other woman puts her foot out and rests it on the stool just to try how it feels, and drawls, "How f-u-n-n-y!"

It is grandmother's stool, that the child used to sit on.

The wagon chest was found and broken open just before the thatch caught fire, by three private soldiers, and they divided the money between them; one spent his share in drink, another had his stolen from him, but the third sent his home to England to a girl in the East End of London.

With part of it she bought a gold brooch and earrings, and the rest she saved to buy a silk wedding dress when he came home.

A syndicate of Jews in Johannesburg and London have bought the farm. They purchased it from the English government, because they think to find gold on it. They have purchased it and paid for it . . . but they do not possess it.

Only the men who lie in their quiet graves upon the hillside, who lived on it, and loved it, possess it; and the piles of stones above them, from among the long waving grasses, keep watch over the land.

The Rooinek

H. C. Bosman

ROOINEKS, said Oom Schalk Lourens, are queer. For instance, there was that day when my nephew Hannes and I had dealings with a couple of Englishmen near Dewetsdorp. It was shortly after Sanna's Post, and Hannes and I were lying behind a rock watching the road. Hannes spent odd moments like that in what he called a useful way. He would file the points of his Mauser cartridges on a piece of flat stone until the lead showed through the steel, in that way making them into dumdum bullets.

I often spoke to my nephew Hannes about that.

"Hannes," I used to say. "That is a sin. The Lord is looking at you."

"That's all right," Hannes replied. "The Lord knows that this is the Boer War, and in wartime he will always forgive a little foolishness like this, especially as the English are so many."

H. C. BOSMAN (1905–1951) was a school teacher and a journalist, and ran his own printing press. He lived overseas for most of a decade and spent a number of years on death row for the shooting death of his stepbrother. Bosman is known for his short stories about rural Afrikaner life, which draw the reader into a peculiar, often tragic world.

Anyway, as we lay behind that rock we saw, far down the road, two horsemen come galloping up. We remained perfectly still and let them approach to within four hundred paces. They were English officers. They were mounted on first-rate horses and their uniforms looked very fine and smart. They were the most stylish-looking men I had seen for some time, and I felt quite ashamed of my own ragged trousers and veldskoens. I was glad that I was behind a rock and they couldn't see me. Especially as my jacket was also torn all the way down the back, as a result of my having had, three days before, to get through a barbed-wire fence rather quickly. I just got through in time, too. The veldkornet, who was a fat man and couldn't run so fast, was about twenty yards behind me. And he remained on the wire with a bullet through him. All through the Boer War I was pleased that I was thin and never troubled with corns.

Hannes and I fired just about the same time. One of the officers fell off his horse. He struck the road with his shoulders and rolled over twice, kicking up the red dust as he turned. Then the other soldier did a queer thing. He drew up his horse and got off. He gave just one look in our direction. Then he led his horse up to where the other man was twisting and struggling on the ground. It took him a little while to lift him on to his horse, for it is no easy matter to pick up a man like that when he is helpless. And he did all this slowly and calmly, as though he was not concerned about the fact that the men who had shot his friend were lying only a few hundred yards away. He managed in some way to support the wounded man across the saddle, and walked on beside the horse. After going a few yards he stopped and seemed to remember something. He turned round and waved at the spot where he imagined we were hiding, as though inviting us to shoot. During all that time I had simply lain watching him, astonished at his coolness.

But when he waved his hand I thrust another cartridge into the breach of my Martini and aimed. At that distance I couldn't miss. I aimed very carefully and was just on the point of pulling the trigger when Hannes put his hand on the barrel and pushed up my rifle.

"Don't shoot, Oom Schalk," he said. "That's a brave man."

I looked at Hannes in surprise. His face was very white. I said nothing, and allowed my rifle to sink down on to the grass, but I couldn't understand what had come over my nephew. It seemed that not only was that Englishman queer, but that Hannes was also queer. That's all nonsense not killing a man just because he's brave. If he's a brave man and he's fighting on the wrong side, that's all the more reason to shoot him.

I was with my nephew Hannes for another few months after that. Then one day, in a skirmish near the Vaal River, Hannes with a few dozen other burghers was cut off from the commando and had to surrender. That was the last I ever saw of him. I heard later on that, after taking him prisoner, the English searched Hannes and found dumdum bullets in his possession. They shot him for that. I was very much grieved when I heard of Hannes's death. He had always been full of life and high spirits. Perhaps Hannes was right in saying that the Lord didn't mind about a little foolishness like dumdum bullets. But the mistake he made was in forgetting that the English did mind.

I was in the veld until they made peace. Then we laid down our rifles and went home. What I knew my farm by was the hole under the koppie where I quarried slate-stones for the threshing floor. That was about all that remained as I left it. Everything else was gone. My home was burnt down. My lands were laid waste. My cattle and sheep were slaughtered. Even the stones I had piled for the kraals were pulled down. My wife came out of the concentration camp, and we went together to look at our old farm. My wife had gone into the concentration camp with our two children, but she came out alone. And when I saw her again and noticed the way she had changed, I knew that I, who had been through all the fighting, had not seen the Boer War.

Neither Sannie nor I had the heart to go on farming again on that same place. It would be different without the children playing about the house and getting into mischief. We got paid out some money by the new government for part of our losses. So I bought a wagon and oxen and left the Free State, which was not even the Free State any longer. It was now called the Orange River Colony.

We trekked right through the Transvaal into the northern part of the Marico Bushveld. Years ago, as a boy, I had trekked through that same country with my parents. Now that I went there again I felt that it was still a good country. It was on the far side of the Dwarsberge, near Derdepoort, that we got a government farm. Afterward other farmers trekked in there as well. One or two of them had also come from the Free State, and I knew them. There were also a few Cape rebels whom I had seen on commando. All of us had lost relatives in the war. Some had died in the concentration camps or on the battlefield. Others had been shot for going into rebellion. So, taken all in all, we who had trekked into that part of the Marico that lay nearest the Bechuanaland border were very bitter against the English.

Then it was that the rooinek came.

It was in the first year of our having settled around Derdepoort. We heard that an Englishman had bought a farm next to Gerhardus Grobbelaar. This was when we were sitting in the voorkamer of Willem Odendaal's house, which was used as a post office. Once a week the post-cart came up with letters from Zeerust, and we came together at Willem Odendaal's house and talked and smoked and drank coffee. Very few of us ever got letters, and then it was mostly demands to pay for the boreholes that had been drilled on our farms or for cement and fencing materials. But every week regularly we went for the post. Sometimes the post-cart didn't come, because the Groen River was in flood, and we would most of us have gone home without noticing it, if somebody didn't speak about it.

When Koos Steyn heard that an Englishman was coming to live amongst us he got up from the riempies-bank.

"No, kêrels," he said. "Always when the Englishman comes, it means that a little later the Boer has got to shift. I'll pack up my wagon and make coffee, and just trek first thing tomorrow morning."

Most of us laughed then. Koos Steyn often said funny

things like that. But some didn't laugh. Somehow, there seemed to be too much truth in Koos Steyn's words.

We discussed the matter and decided that if we Boers in the Marico could help it the rooinek would not stay amongst us too long. About half an hour later one of Willem Odendaal's children came in and said that there was a strange wagon coming along the big road. We went to the door and looked out. As the wagon came nearer we saw that it was piled up with all kinds of furniture and also sheets of iron and farming implements. There was so much stuff on the wagon that the tent had to be taken off to get everything on.

The wagon rolled along and came to a stop in front of the house. With the wagon there were one white man and two kaffirs. The white man shouted something to the kaffirs and threw down the whip. Then he walked up to where we were standing. He was dressed just as we were, in shirt and trousers and veldskoens, and he had dust all over him. But when he stepped over a thornbush we saw that he had got socks on. Therefore we knew that he was an Englishman.

Koos Steyn was standing in front of the door.

The Englishman went up to him and held out his hand.

"Good afternoon," he said in Afrikaans. "My name is Webber."

Koos shook hands with him.

"My name is Prince Lord Alfred Milner," Koos Steyn said.

That was when Lord Milner was governor of the Transvaal, and we all laughed. The rooinek also laughed.

"Well, Lord Prince," he said, "I can speak your language a little, and I hope that later on I'll be able to speak it better. I'm coming to live here, and I hope that we'll all be friends."

He then came round to all of us, but the others turned away and refused to shake hands with him. He came up to me last of all; I felt sorry for him, and although his nation had dealt unjustly with my nation, and I had lost both my children in the concentration camp, still it was not so much the fault of this Englishman. It was the fault of the English government, who wanted our gold mines. And it was also the fault of Queen Victoria, who didn't like Oom Paul Kruger, because they say that when he went over to London, Oom Paul spoke to her only once for a few minutes. Oom Paul Kruger said that he was a married man and he was afraid of widows.

When the Englishman Webber went back to his wagon Koos Steyn and I walked with him. He told us that he had bought the farm next to Gerhardus Grobbelaar and that he didn't know much about sheep and cattle and mealies, but he had bought a few books on farming, and he was going to learn all he could out of them. When he said that, I looked away toward the poort. I didn't want him to see that I was laughing. But with Koos Steyn it was otherwise.

"Man," he said, "let me see those books."

Webber opened the box at the bottom of the wagon and took out about six big books with green covers.

"These are very good books," Koos Steyn said. "Yes, they are very good for the white ants. The white ants will eat them all in two nights."

As I have told you, Koos Steyn was a funny fellow, and no man could help laughing at the things he said.

Those were bad times. There was drought, and we could not sow mealies. The dams dried up, and there was only last year's grass on the veld. We had to pump water out of the borehole for weeks at a time. Then the rains came and for a while things were better.

Now and again I saw Webber. From what I heard about him it seemed that he was working hard. But of course no rooinek can make a living out of farming, unless they send him money every month from England. And we found out that almost all the money Webber had was what he had paid on the farm. He was always reading in those green books what he had to do. It's lucky that those books are written in English, and that the Boers can't read them. Otherwise many more farmers would be ruined every year. When his cattle had the heartwater, or his sheep had the bluetongue, or there were cutworms or stalk-borers in his mealies, Webber would look it all up in his books. I suppose that when the kaffirs stole his sheep he would look that up too.

Still, Koos Steyn helped Webber quite a lot and taught him a number of things, so that matters did not go as badly with him as they would have if he had only acted according to the lies that were printed in those green books. Webber and Koos Steyn became very friendly. Koos Steyn's wife had had a baby just a few weeks before Webber came. It was the first child they had after being married seven years, and they were very proud of it. It was a girl. Koos Steyn said that he would sooner it had been a boy; but that, even so, it was better than nothing. Right from the first Webber had taken a liking to that child, who was christened Jemima after her mother. Often when I passed Koos Steyn's house I saw the Englishman sitting on the front stoep with the child on his knees.

In the meantime the other farmers around there became annoyed on account of Koos Steyn's friendship with the rooinek. They said that Koos was a hendsopper and a traitor to his country. He was intimate with a man who had helped to bring about the downfall of the Afrikaner nation. Yet it was not fair to call Koos a hendsopper. Koos had lived in the Graaff-Reinet District when the war broke out, so that he was a Cape Boer and need not have fought. Nevertheless, he joined up with a Free State commando and remained until peace was made, and if at any time the English had caught him they would have shot him as a rebel, in the same way that they shot Scheepers and many others.

Gerhardus Grobbelaar spoke about this once when we were in Willem Odendaal's post office.

"You are not doing right," Gerhardus said, "Boer and Englishman have been enemies since before Slagtersnek. We've lost this war, but some day we'll win. It's the duty we owe to our children's children to stand against the rooineks. Remember the concentration camps."

There seemed to me to be truth in what Gerhardus said.

"But the English are here now, and we've got to live with them," Koos answered. "When we get to understand one another perhaps we won't need to fight any more. This Englishman Webber is learning Afrikaans very well, and some day he might almost be one of us. The only thing

I can't understand about him is that he has a bath every morning. But if he stops that and if he doesn't brush his teeth any more you will hardly be able to tell him from a Boer."

Although he made a joke about it, I felt that in what Koos Steyn said there was also truth.

Then, the year after the drought, the miltsiek broke out. The miltsiek seemed to be in the grass of the veld, and in the water of the dams, and even in the air the cattle breathed. All over the place I would find cows and oxen lying dead. We all became very discouraged. Nearly all of us in that part of the Marico had started farming again on what the government had given us. Now that the stock died we had nothing. First the drought had put us back to where we were when we started. Now with the miltsiek we couldn't hope to do anything. We couldn't even sow mealies, because, at the rate at which the cattle were dying, in a short while we would have no oxen left to pull the plow. People talked of selling what they had and going to look for work on the gold mines. We sent a petition to the government, but that did no good.

It was then that somebody got hold of the idea of trekking. In a few days we were talking of nothing else. But the question was where we could trek to. They would not allow us into Rhodesia for fear we might spread the miltsiek there as well. And it was useless going to any other part of the Transvaal. Somebody mentioned German West Africa. We had none of us been there before, and I suppose that really was the reason why, in the end, we decided to go there.

"The blight of the English is over South Africa," Gerhardus Grobbelaar said. "We'll remain here only to die. We must go away somewhere where there is not the Englishman's flag."

In a few weeks' time we arranged everything. We were going to trek across the Kalahari into German territory. Everything we had we loaded up. We drove the cattle ahead and followed behind on our wagons. There were five families: the Steyns, the Grobbelaars, the Odendaals, the Ferreiras and Sannie and I. Webber also came with us. I think it was not so much that he was anxious to leave as that he and Koos Steyn had become very much attached to one another, and the Englishman did not wish to remain alone behind.

The youngest person in our trek was Koos Steyn's daughter Jemima, who was then about eighteen months old. Being the baby, she was a favorite with all of us.

Webber sold his wagon and went with Koos Steyn's trek.

When at the end of the first day we outspanned several miles inside the Bechuanaland Protectorate, we were very pleased that we were done with the Transvaal, where we had had so much misfortune. Of course, the Protectorate was also British territory, but all the same we felt happier there than we had done in our country. We saw Webber every day now, and although he was a foreigner with strange ways, and would remain an uitlander until he died, yet we disliked him less than before for being a rooinek.

It was on the first Sunday that we reached Malopolole. For the first part of our way the country remained Bushveld. There were the same kind of thorn trees that grew in the Marico, except that they became fewer the deeper into the Kalahari that we went. Also, the ground became more and more sandy, until even before we came to Malopolole it was all desert. But scattered thornbushes remained all the way. That Sunday we held a religious service. Gerhardus Grobbelaar read a chapter out of the Bible and offered up a prayer. We sang a number of psalms, after which Gerhardus prayed again. I shall always remember that Sunday and the way we sat on the ground beside one of the wagons, listening to Gerhardus. That was the last Sunday that we were all together.

The Englishman sat next to Koos Steyn and the baby Jemima lay down in front of him. She played with Webber's fingers and tried to bite them. It was funny to watch her. Several times Webber looked down at her and smiled. I thought then that although Webber was not one of us, yet Jemima certainly did not know it. Maybe in a thing like that the child was wiser than we were. To her it made no difference that the man whose fingers she bit was born in another country and did not speak the same language that she did.

There are many things that I remember about that trek into the Kalahari. But one thing that now seems strange to me is the way in which, right from the first day, we took Gerhardus Grobbelaar for our leader. Whatever he said we just seemed to do without talking very much about it. We all felt that it was right simply because Gerhardus wished it. That was a strange thing about our trek. It was not simply that we knew Gerhardus had got the Lord with him—for we did know that—but it was rather that we believed in Gerhardus as well as in the Lord. I think that even if Gerhardus Grobbelaar had been an ungodly man we would still have followed him in exactly the same way. For when you are in the desert and there is no water and the way back is long, then you feel that it is better to have with you a strong man who does not read the Book very much, than a man who is good and religious, and yet does not seem sure how far to trek each day and where to outspan.

But Gerhardus Grobbelaar was a man of God. At the same time there was something about him that made you feel that it was only by acting as he advised that you could succeed. There was only one other man I have ever known who found it so easy to get people to do as he wanted. And that was Paul Kruger. He was very much like Gerhardus Grobbelaar, except that Gerhardus was less quarrelsome. But of the two Paul Kruger was the bigger man.

Only once do I remember Gerhardus losing his temper. And that was with the Nagmaal at Elandsberg. It was on a Sunday, and we were camped out beside the Crocodile River. Gerhardus went round early in the morning from wagon to wagon and told us that he wanted everybody to come over to where his wagon stood. The Lord had been good to us at that time, so that we had had much rain and our cattle were fat. Gerhardus explained that he wanted to hold a service, to thank the Lord for all His good works, but more especially for what He had done for the farmers of the northern part of the Groot Marico District. This was a good plan, and we all came together with our Bibles and hymnbooks. But one man, Karel Pieterse, remained behind at his wagon. Twice Gerhardus went to call him, but Karel Pieterse lay down on the grass and would not get up to come to the service. He said it was all right thanking the Lord now that there had been rains, but what about all those seasons when there had been drought and the cattle had died of thirst. Gerhardus Grobbelaar shook his head sadly, and said there was nothing he could do then, as it was Sunday. But he prayed that the Lord would soften Brother Pieterse's heart, and he finished off his prayer by saying that in any case, in the morning, he would help to soften the brother's heart himself.

The following morning Gerhardus walked over with a sjambok and an ox-riem to where Karel Pieterse sat before his fire, watching the kaffir making coffee. They were both of them men who were big in the body. But Gerhardus got the better of the struggle. In the end he won. He fastened Karel to the wheel of his own wagon with the ox-riem. Then he thrashed him with the sjambok while Karel's wife and children were looking on.

That had happened years before. But nobody had forgotten. And now, in the Kalahari, when Gerhardus summoned us to a service, it was noticed that no man stayed away.

Just outside Malopolole is a muddy stream that is dry part of the year and part of the year has a foot or so of brackish water. We were lucky in being there just at the time when it had water. Early the following morning we filled up the water barrels that we had put on our wagons before leaving the Marico. We were going right into the desert, and we did not know where we would get water again. Even the Bakwena kaffirs could not tell us for sure.

"The Great Dorstland Trek," Koos Steyn shouted as we

got ready to move off. "Anyway, we won't fare as badly as the Dorstland Trekkers. We'll lose less cattle than they did because we've got less to lose. And seeing that we are only five families, not more than about a dozen of us will die of thirst."

I thought it was bad luck for Koos Steyn to make jokes like that about the Dorstland Trek, and I think that others felt the same way about it. We trekked right through that day, and it was all desert. By sunset we had not come across a sign of water anywhere. Abraham Ferreira said toward evening that perhaps it would be better if we went back to Malopolole and tried to find out for sure which was the best way of getting through the Kalahari. But the rest said that there was no need to do that, since we would be sure to come across water the next day. And, anyway, we were Doppers and, having once set out, we were not going to turn back. But after we had given the cattle water our barrels did not have too much left in them.

By the middle of the following day all our water had given out except a little that we kept for the children. But still we pushed on. Now that we had gone so far we were afraid to go back because of the long way that we would have to go without water to get back to Malopolole. In the evening we were very anxious. We all knelt down in the sand and prayed. Gerhardus Grobbelaar's voice sounded very deep and earnest when he besought God to have mercy on us, especially for the sakes of the little ones. He mentioned the baby Jemima by name. The Englishman knelt down beside me, and I noticed that he shivered when Gerhardus mentioned Koos Steyn's child.

It was moonlight. All around us was the desert. Our

wagons seemed very small and lonely; there was something about them that looked very mournful. The women and children put their arms round one another and wept a long while. Our kaffirs stood some distance away and watched us. My wife Sannie put her hand in mine, and I thought of the concentration camp. Poor woman, she had suffered much. And I knew that her thoughts were the same as my own: that after all it was perhaps better that our children should have died then than now.

We had got so far into the desert that we began telling one another that we must be near the end. Although we knew that German West was far away, and that in the way we had been traveling we had got little more than into the beginning of the Kalahari, yet we tried to tell one another lies about how near water was likely to be. But, of course, we told those lies only to one another. Each man in his own heart knew what the real truth was. And later on we even stopped telling one another lies about what a good chance we had of getting out alive. You can understand how badly things had gone with us when you know that we no longer troubled about hiding our position from the women and children. They wept, some of them. But that made no difference then. Nobody tried to comfort the women and children who cried. We knew that tears were useless, and yet somehow at that hour we felt that the weeping of the women was not less useless than the courage of the men. After a while, there was no more weeping in our camp. Some of the women who lived through the dreadful things of the days that came after and got safely back to the Transvaal, never again wept. What they had seen appeared to have hardened them. In this respect they had become as men. I think that is the saddest thing that ever happens in this world, when women pass through great suffering that makes them become as men.

That night we hardly slept. Early the next morning the men went out to look for water. An hour after sun-up Ferreira came back and told us that he had found a muddy pool a few miles away. We all went there, but there wasn't much water. Still, we got a little, and that made us feel better. It was only when it came to driving our cattle toward the mudhole that we found our kaffirs had deserted us during the night. After we had gone to sleep they had stolen away. Some of the weaker cattle couldn't get up to go to the pool. So we left them. Some were trampled to death or got choked in the mud, and we had to pull them out to let the rest get to the hole. It was pitiful.

Just before we left, one of Ferreira's daughters died. We scooped a hole in the sand and buried her.

So we decided to trek back.

After his daughter was dead Abraham Ferreira went up to Gerhardus and told him that if we had taken his advice earlier on and gone back, his daughter would not have died.

"Your daughter is dead now, Abraham," Gerhardus said. "It is no use talking about her any longer. We all have to die some day. I refused to go back earlier. I have decided to go back now."

Abraham Ferreira looked Gerhardus in the eyes and laughed. I shall always remember how that laughter sounded in the desert. In Abraham's voice there was the hoarseness of the sand and thirst. His voice was cracked with what the desert had done to him; his face was lined and his lips were blackened. But there was nothing about him that spoke of grief for his daughter's death.

"Your daughter is still alive, Oom Gerhardus," Abraham Ferreira said, pointing to the wagon wherein lay Gerhardus's wife, who was weak, and the child to whom she had given birth only a few months before. "Yes, she is still alive . . . so far."

Ferreira turned away laughing, and we heard him a little later explaining to his wife in cracked tones about the joke he had made.

Gerhardus Grobbelaar merely watched the other man walk away without saying anything. So far we had followed Gerhardus through all things, and our faith in him had been great. But now that we had decided to trek back we lost our belief in him. We lost it suddenly, too. We knew that it was best to turn back, and that to continue would mean that we would all die in the Kalahari. And yet, if Gerhardus had said we must still go on we would have done so. We would have gone through with him right to the end. But now that he as much as said he was beaten by the desert we had no more faith in Gerhardus. That is why I have said that Paul Kruger was a greater man than Gerhardus. Because Paul Kruger was that kind of man whom we still worshipped even when he decided to retreat. If it had been Paul Kruger who told us that we had to go back we would have returned with strong hearts. We would have retained exactly the same love for our leader, even if we knew that he was beaten. But from the moment that Gerhardus said we must go back we all knew that he was no longer our leader. Gerhardus knew that also.

We knew what lay between us and Malopolole and there was grave doubt in our hearts when we turned our wagons round. Our cattle were very weak, and we had to inspan all that could walk. We hadn't enough yokes, and therefore we cut poles from the scattered bushes and tied them to the trek-chains. As we were also without skeis we had to fasten the necks of the oxen straight on to the yokes with strops, and several of the oxen got strangled.

Then we saw that Koos Steyn had become mad. For he refused to return. He inspanned his oxen and got ready to trek on. His wife sat silent in the wagon with the baby; wherever her husband went she would go, too. That was only right, of course. Some women kissed her goodbye, and cried. But Koos Steyn's wife did not cry. We reasoned with Koos about it, but he said that he had made up his mind to cross the Kalahari, and he was not going to turn back just for nonsense.

"But, man," Gerhardus Grobbelaar said to him, "you've got no water to drink."

"I'll drink coffee then," Koos Steyn answered, laughing as always, and took up the whip and walked away beside the wagon. And Webber went off with him, just because Koos Steyn had been good to him, I suppose. That's why I have said that Englishmen are queer. Webber must have known that if Koos Steyn had not actually gone wrong in the head, still what he was doing now was madness, and yet he stayed with him.

We separated. Our wagons went slowly back to Malopolole. Koos Steyn's wagon went deeper into the desert. My wagon went last. I looked back at the Steyns. At that moment Webber also looked round. He saw me

and waved his hand. It reminded me of that day in the
Boer War when that other Englishman, whose companion we had shot, also turned round and waved.

Eventually we got back to Malopolole with two wagons
and a handful of cattle. We abandoned the other wagons.
Awful things happened on that desert. A number of children died. Gerhardus Grobbelaar's wagon was in front of
me. Once I saw a bundle being dropped through the side
of the wagon-tent. I knew what it was. Gerhardus would
not trouble to bury his dead child, and his wife lay in the
tent too weak to move. So I got off the wagon and scraped
a small heap of sand over the body. All I remember of the
rest of the journey to Malopolole is the sun and the sand.
And the thirst. Although at one time we thought that we
had lost our way, yet that did not matter much to us. We
were past feeling. We could neither pray nor curse, our
parched tongues cleaving to the roofs of our mouths.

Until today I am not sure how many days we were on
our way back, unless I sit down and work it all out, and
then I suppose I get it wrong. We got back to Malopolole
and water. We said we would never go away from there
again. I don't think that even those parents who had lost
children grieved about them then. They were stunned with
what they had gone through. But I knew that later on it
would all come back again. Then they would remember
things about shallow graves in the sand, and Gerhardus
Grobbelaar and his wife would think of a little bundle
lying out in the Kalahari. And I knew how they would
feel.

Afterward we fitted out a wagon with fresh oxen; we
took an abundant supply of water and went back into the

desert to look for the Steyn family. With the help of the Sechuana kaffirs, who could see tracks that we could not see, we found the wagon. The oxen had been outspanned; a few lay dead beside the wagon. The kaffirs pointed out to us footprints on the sand, which showed which way those two men and that woman had gone.

In the end we found them.

Koos Steyn and his wife lay side by side in the sand; the woman's head rested on the man's shoulder; her long hair had become loosened, and blew about softly in the wind. A great deal of fine sand had drifted over their bodies. Near them the Englishman lay, face downwards. We never found the baby Jemima. She must have died somewhere along the way and Koos Steyn must have buried her. But we agreed that the Englishman Webber must have passed through terrible things; he could not even have had any understanding left as to what the Steyns had done with their baby. He probably thought, up to the moment when he died, that he was carrying the child. For, when we lifted his body, we found, still clasped in his dead and rigid arms, a few old rags and a child's clothes.

It seemed to us that the wind that always stirs in the Kalahari blew very quietly and softly that morning.

Yes, the wind blew very gently.

Nokulunga's Wedding

Gcina Mhlope

MOUNT FRERE was one of the worst places for a woman to live. A woman had to marry whoever had enough money for lobola and that was that. Nokulunga was one of many such victims whose parents wholeheartedly agreed to their victimization. She became wife to Xolani Mayeza.

By the time Nokulunga was sixteen years old she was already looking her best. One day a number of young men came to the river where she and her friends used to fetch water. The men were strangers. As the girls came to the river, one of the men jumped very high and cried in a high-pitched voice.

"Hayi, hayi, hayi!

Bri—bri mntanam uyagula!"

He came walking in style toward the girls and asked for water. After drinking he thanked them, went back

GCINA MHLOPE (1960–). A stage and screen performer, Mhlope has authored short fiction, poems, and plays for adults as well as stories for children and championed storytelling as a way of keeping history alive. She holds honorary doctorates from the London Open University and the University of KwaZulu-Natal.

to his friends and they left. This was not a new thing to Nokulunga and her friends, but the different clothes and style of walking left them with mixed feelings. Some were very impressed by the strangers but Nokulunga was not. She suspected they were up to something but decided not to worry about people she did not know. The girls lifted their water pots onto their heads and went home.

In late February the same strange men were seen at the river, but their number had doubled. The day was very hot but they were dressed in heavy overcoats. Nokulunga did not see them until she and her friends were near the river. The girls were happily arguing about something and did not recognize the men as the same ones they had seen before. Only when the same man who had asked for water came up to them again did they realize who the strangers were. Nokulunga began to feel uneasy.

He drank all his water slowly this time, then he asked Nokulunga if he could take her home with him for the night. She was annoyed, and filled her water pot, balanced it on her head, and told the others she had to hurry home. One of her friends did the same and was ready to go with Nokulunga when the other men came and barred their way.

Things began to happen very fast. They took Nokulunga's water pot and broke it on a rock. Men wrapped Nokulunga in big overcoats before she could scream. They slung the bundle onto their shoulders.

The other girls helplessly looked on as the men set off. The men chanted a traditional wedding song as they quickly climbed the hillside, while many villagers watched.

Nokulunga twisted round, trying to breathe. She had witnessed girls being taken before. She thought of the many people in the neighborhood who seemed to love her. They couldn't love her if they could let strangers go away with her without putting up a fight. She felt betrayed and lost. She thought of what she had heard about such marriages. She knew her mother would not mind, as long as the man had enough lobola.

The journey was long and she was very hot inside the big coats. Her body felt so heavy, but the rhythm of her carriers went on and on . . . Her lover Vuyo was going back to Germiston to work. He had promised her that he would be away for seven months then he would be back to marry her. She had been so happy.

Her carriers were walking down a very steep and uneven path. Soon she heard people talking and dogs barking. She was put down and the bundle was unwrapped. A lot of people were looking on to see what the newcomer looked like. She was clumsily helped to her feet and stood there stupidly for viewing. She wanted to pee. For a while no one said anything; they all stood there with different expressions on their faces. The children of the house came in to join the viewing one by one and the small hut was nearly full.

She was in Xolani, her "husband's" room. She was soon left alone with him for the night. She sat down calmly, giving no indication that she was going to sleep at all. Xolani tried to chat with her but she was silent, so he got undressed and into the big bed on the floor. He coughed a few times, then uneasily invited her to join him. She sat silent. He was quiet for a while, then asked if she was going to sleep that night. No. For a long time she sat staring at him. She was watchful.

But Nokulunga was tired. She thought he was sleeping. Xolani suddenly lunged and grabbed her arm. His eyes were strange, she could not make out what was in them, anger or hatred or something else.

She struggled to free her arm; he suddenly let go and she fell. She quickly stood up, still watching him. He smiled and moved close to her. She backed off. It looked like a game, he following her slowly, she backing round and round the room. Each round they moved faster. Xolani decided he had had enough and grabbed her again. She was about to scream when he covered her mouth. She realized it was foolish to scream; it would call helpers for him.

She still stood a chance of winning if they were alone. He was struggling to undress her when Nokulunga went for his arm. She dug her teeth deep and tore a piece of flesh out. She spat. His arm went limp, he groaned and sat, gritting his teeth and holding his arm.

Nokulunga sat too, breathing heavily. He stood up quickly, cursing under his breath and kicked her as hard as he could. She whined with pain but did not stand up to defend herself.

Blood was dripping from Xolani's arm and he softly ordered her to tear a piece of sheet to tie above the bite. She did it, then wiped blood from the floor. Xolani got under the bedcovers in silence. Nokulunga pulled her clothes together. She did not dare to fall asleep. Whether Xolani slept or not, only he knows. The pain of his arm did not make things easier for him.

Day came. Xolani left, and Nokulunga was given a plate of food and locked in the room. She had just started eating when she heard people talking outside. It sounded like a lot of men. They went into the hut next to the one she was in and came out talking even louder. They moved away and she gave up listening and ate her food, soft porridge.

The men sat next to the big cattle-kraal. Xolani was there, his father Malunga and his eldest brother Diniso. The rest were uncles and other family members. They were slowly drinking their beer. They were all very angry with Xolani. Malunga was too angry to think straight. He looked at his son with contempt, kept balling his hands into fists.

No one said anything. They stole quick glances at Malunga and their eyes went back to stare at the ground. Xolani shifted uneasily. He was holding his hurt arm carefully; his uncle had tended to it but the pain was still there. His father sucked at his pipe, knocked it out on the piece of wood next to him, then spat between his teeth. The saliva jumped a long way into the kraal and they all watched it.

"Xolani!" Malunga called to his son softly and angrily.

"Yes father," Xolani replied without looking up.

"What are you telling us, are you telling us that you spent all night with that girl and failed to sleep with her?"

"Father, I . . . I . . ."

"Yes, you failed to be a man with that girl in that hut. That is the kind of man you have grown into, unable to sleep with a woman the way a man should."

Silence followed. No one dared to look at Malunga. He busied himself refilling his pipe as if he was alone. After lighting it he looked at the other men.

"Diniso, are you listening with me to what your brother is telling us? Tell us more Xolani, what else did she do to you, my little boy? Did she kick you on the chest too, tell me, father's little son?" He laughed harshly.

An old man interrupted. "Mocking and laughing at the fool will not solve our problem. So please, everyone think of the next step from here. The Mjakuja people are looking for their daughter. Something must be done fast." He was out of breath when he finished. The old man was Malunga's father from another house.

The problem was that no word had been sent to Nokulunga's family to tell them of her whereabouts. Thirteen cattle and a well-fed horse were ready to be taken to the family, along with a goat which was called imvulamlomo, mouth opener.

The sun was about to set. Nokulunga watched it for a long time. She was very quiet. She stared at the red orange shape as it went down into the unknown side of the mountain.

By the time the colors faded she was still looking at the same spot but her eyes were taking a look at her future. She had not escaped that day. She felt weak and miserable. A group of boys sat all day on the nearby hill watching her so that she did not try running away. She was there to stay.

She did not know how long she stood there behind the hut. She only came to when she heard a little girl laughing next to her. The girl told her that people had gone out to look for her because they all thought she had managed to get away while the boys were playing. She went back into the house. Her mother-in-law and the other women also laughed when the little girl said she'd found Nokulunga standing behind the hut. More boys were sent to tell the pursuers that Nokulunga was safe at home.

She hated the long dress and doek she had been given to wear; they were too big for her and the material still had the hard starch on it. The people who had gone out to look for her came back laughing and teasing each other about how stupid they had been to run so fast without even checking behind the house first.

Nokulunga was trembling as it grew dark. She knew things would not be as easy as they had been the night before. She knew the family would take further steps although she did not know exactly what would happen.

She was in her husband's room waiting for him to come in. The hut suddenly looked so small she felt it move to enclose her in a painful death. She held her arms across her chest, gripping her shoulders so tight they ached.

The door opened and a number of men about her husband's age came in quietly. They closed the door behind them. She watched Xolani undress as if he did not want to. His arm did not look better as he stood there in the light of the low-burning paraffin lamp. She started to cry.

She was held and undressed. Her face was wet with sweat and tears and she wanted to go and pee. The men laughed a little.

One of them smiled teasingly at her and ordered her to lie down on the bed. She cried uncontrollably when she saw the look on Xolani's face. He stood there with eyes wide open as if he was walking in dreamland, his face had the expression of a lost and helpless boy. Was that the man she was supposed to look upon as a husband? How was he ever to defend her against anything or anyone?

Hands pulled her up and her streaming eyes did not see the man who shouted to her that she should lie like a woman. She wiped her eyes and saw Xolani approaching her.

She jumped and pushed him away, grabbed at her clothes. The group of men was on her like a mob. They roughly pulled her back onto the bed and Xolani was placed on top of her. Her legs were each pulled by a man. Others held her arms.

Men were cheering and clapping hands while Xolani jumped high, now enjoying the rape. One man was saying that he had had enough of holding the leg and wanted a share for his work. Things were said too about her bloody thighs and she heard roars of laughter before she fainted.

> *The bride is ours*
> *The bride is ours*
> *Mother will never go to sleep*
> *without food*
> *without food*
> *The bride is ours*
> *The bride is ours*
> *Father will never need for beer*
> *will never want for beer . . .*

The young men were singing near the kraal. Girls giggled as they sang and did Xhosa dances. Soon they would be expected to dance at Xolani's wedding. They were trying new hairstyles so each would look her best. The young men too were worried about how they would look. Some of them were hoping for new relationships with the girls of Gudlintaba. That place was known for the good-looking girls with their beautiful voices. Others knew too that some relationships would break as a result of that wedding. Everyone knew the day was in their hands, whether fighting or laughter ended the day.

Women prepared beer and took turns going to the river for water, happy and light-footed in the way they walked. Time and again a woman would run from hut to hut calling at the top of her voice, ululating joyfully:

"Lilililili . . . lili . . . lili . . . liiiiii!

To give birth is to stretch your bones!

What do you say, woman who never gave birth?"

Nokulunga spent most of the time inside the house with one of her friends and her mother's sister tending to her face. They had a mixture of eggs and tree barks as part of the concoction. All day long her face was crusted with thick liquids supposed to be good for her wedding complexion. Time and again her mother's sister would sit down and tell her how to behave now that she was a woman. How she hated the subject. She wished days would simply go by without her noticing them.

"Ingwe iyawavula amathambo 'mqolo.

The leopard opens the back bones."

She heard the girls happily singing outside. She hated the bloody song. The only thing they all seemed to care about was the food they were going to have on that day she never wanted to come. Many times she would find herself sitting there with her masked face looking out of the tiny window. She hated Xolani and his name. She felt that he was given that name because he would always do things to hurt people, then he would keep on apologizing and explaining. Xolani means "please forgive."

The day came. Nokulunga walked slowly by Xolani's side with lots of singing and laughing and ululating and clapping of hands around her. She did not smile; when she tried only tears came rolling down to make her ashamed.

It was the day of his life for Xolani, such a beautiful wife and such a big wedding. He was smiling and squeezing her hand when Nokulunga saw Vuyo. He was looking at Xolani with loathing, his fists very tight and his lips so hard. She pulled her hand from Xolani's and took a few steps. She began to cry. Xolani went to her and tried to comfort her. A lot of people saw this, they stood watching and sympathizing and wondering . . .

Months passed. Nokulunga was sitting by the fire, in her arms a five-day-old baby boy was sleeping so peacefully she smiled. Her father-in-law had named it Vuyo. How thankful she had been to hear that; she would always remember the old Vuyo she had loved.

Nokulunga now accepted that Xolani was her lifetime partner and there was nothing she could do about it. Once she saw Vuyo in town and they had kissed. It had been clear to them that since she was already pregnant, she was Xolani's wife, and Vuyo knew he would have to pay a lot of cattle if he took Nokulunga with the unborn baby. There was nothing to be done.

Episodes in the Rural Areas

Modikwe Dikobe

I

"BAAS I WANT TO GET MARRIED."

"What do you want me to do for you?"

"To help me with eight head of cattle."

"How will you pay back?"

"I shall work for you until I have recovered their price."

"Alright Jan, I shall advance you eight cattle. Piet will play father for you. Piet see that you get me a receipt. Nothing else must be written on the receipt except eight head of cattle."

Piet herds the bogadi to Jan's parents-in-law. Mary, Jan's bride, accompanies him. She's immediately engaged for domestic chores. Jan is on outdoor duties. During the day Captain Smythe has sexual intercourse with Mary.

MODIKWE DIKOBE (Marks Dikobe Ramitloa) (1913–?) is the author of the celebrated novel *The Marabi Dance* about township life in Johannesburg, which chronicles the clash between city and rural cultures and the advent of new urban identities. First published in 1973, it is considered a seminal work in twentieth-century South African literature.

Jan is told by others who had noticed the boss's misdeeds. Jan deserts the farm in the evening with his wife. Capt. Smythe reports him to the district magistrate. He appears in court for desertion. He is asked to plead.

"Mokolo sleeps with my wife."

The magistrate is astounded.

"What!"

"Yes baas, Mokolo sleeps with my wife."

"Did you not promise to work for him until you've recovered the price of eight head of cattle you paid for bogadi?"

"Yes, but he sleeps with my wife."

The magistrate remained adamant.

"You must go back and work for him."

"Haaikona baas, he sleeps with my wife."

II

On a farm in Rust De Winter are squatters working on option for a farmer. Mr. Mackay has a son primed for farming duties. The only children nearby are squatters' ones.

Mr. Mackay plays with them. On a certain day one of the squatters obediently greets Mr. Mackay.

"Baas, I want to talk to you."

"What is it about, Piet?"

"Young baas has spoiled my daughter."

"What! My son spoiled your daughter? Do you mean he has got your daughter pregnant?"

"Yes, baas. She is in her third month. She says the young baas got her like that."

"Look, Piet. Your kaffir children have been coming

here. Do you think a bull will leave a bitch if it exposes itself? It is your daughter that has spoiled my son. Get out of this place."

III

"Hans, my ox has disappeared. Do you perhaps know who has stolen it?"

"No, baas."

"Have you perhaps sold it as yours by mistake?"

"I sold no ox, baas."

"What about the one slaughtered for your niece's wedding?"

"I have not been to the wedding."

"You're a bad uncle not to attend your niece's wedding."

Hans remains silent.

"I am attending the wedding this afternoon. Will you come with me?"

Hans drops his head.

Mr. Post leaves without Hans. He squats at a beer-drinking group. He asks to see the skin of the slaughtered beast.

"I buy skins," he tells the father of the home.

"The skin is for the uncle of my daughter," he is reminded.

"All right, I will take it home for him."

Mr. Post has it loaded on a horse-cart.

"Hans," he calls out, "I've brought your skin. Come and see it."

Hans comes, his hands folded; avoiding looking at the skin.

"Hans don't worry. I won't call the police on you: Go and fetch sixteen of your oxen. I shall choose one to replace mine."

The sixteen oxen are driven to Mr Post.

"All right, Hans. Thank you. All these sixteen replace mine. You and I are old friends. We don't want police intervention."

IV

Geelbooi and Thomas arrive on a farm late in the afternoon. Thomas is neatly dressed. He looks sophisticated. He seems to be following the farmer as he tells Geelbooi that the sale of livestock is tomorrow. Geelbooi now and then nods foolishly. "Yaa, baas, yaa, baas," he keeps on repeating.

The trouble comes when the farmer asks: "Waar vanaf kom julle?"

"Skilpadfontein," replies Thomas.

"Wat! Nie 'Skilpadfontein baas' nie?"

Geelbooi is shown a hut for night shelter.

"Maar nie vir daardie Engelse kaffir nie."

V

Thomas has not yet received a lesson that this is the Platteland.

"Kaffirs" are not allowed just to speak without respect to a white person. He enters a novelty shop and examines authors' names on the books.

"Hoekom vra jy nie wat jy soek nie?"

"Sorry, madam. I have already found one that I want."

"Ja! Jy praat nog Engels."

"A bit of Afrikaans, too, nooi."

"Wat is jy?"

"An author."

The shopowner changes to English.

"I would like to see what you've written."

A month later Thomas arrives with the book he has written.

"Can I have it for reading?"

The following month, Thomas calls again.

"Your book is down-to-earth. You should add to what happened in the later life of your heroine. She is such a marvelous girl to have braved shame by not discarding her baby."

The Ultimate Safari

Nadine Gordimer

THAT NIGHT OUR MOTHER WENT to the shop and she didn't come back. Ever. What happened? I don't know. My father also had gone away one day and never come back; but he was fighting in the war. We were in the war, too, but we were children, we were like our grandmother and grandfather, we didn't have guns. The people my father was fighting—the bandits, they are called by our government—ran all over the place and we ran away from them like chickens chased by dogs. We didn't know where to go. Our mother went to the shop because someone said you could get some oil for cooking. We were happy because we hadn't tasted oil for a long time; perhaps she got the oil and someone knocked her down in the dark and took that oil from her. Perhaps she met the bandits. If you meet them, they will kill you. Twice they came to our village and we ran and hid in the bush and when they'd gone we came back and found they had taken

---

NADINE GORDIMER (1923–). A prolific novelist and author of short stories, Gordimer has won the Booker Prize, the Commonwealth Writers' Prize for the Africa Region, and the Nobel Prize for literature. Much of her writing concerns the effects of apartheid on human relations.

everything; but the third time they came back there was nothing to take, no oil, no food, so they burned the thatch and the roofs of our houses fell in. My mother found some pieces of tin and we put those up over part of the house. We were waiting there for her that night she never came back.

We were frightened to go out, even to do our business, because the bandits did come. Not into our house—without a roof it must have looked as if there was no one in it, everything gone—but all through the village. We heard people screaming and running. We were afraid even to run, without our mother to tell us where. I am the middle one, the girl, and my little brother clung against my stomach with his arms round my neck and his legs round my waist like a baby monkey to its mother. All night my first-born brother kept in his hand a broken piece of wood from one of our burnt house-poles. It was to save himself if the bandits found him.

We stayed there all day. Waiting for her. I don't know what day it was; there was no school, no church any more in our village, so you didn't know whether it was a Sunday or a Monday.

When the sun was going down, our grandmother and grandfather came. Someone from our village had told them we children were alone, our mother had not come back. I say "grandmother" before "grandfather" because it's like that: our grandmother is big and strong, not yet old, and our grandfather is small, you don't know where he is, in his loose trousers, he smiles but he hasn't heard what you're saying, and his hair looks as if he's left it full of soap suds. Our grandmother took us—me, the baby, my first-born brother, our grandfather—back to her house and we were all afraid (except the baby, asleep on our grandmother's back) of meeting the bandits on the way. We waited a long time at our grandmother's place. Perhaps it was a month. We were hungry. Our mother never came. While we were waiting for her to fetch us our grandmother had no food for us, no food for our grandfather and herself. A woman with milk in her breasts gave us some for my little brother, although at our house he used to eat porridge, same as we did. Our grandmother took us to look for wild spinach but everyone else in her village did the same and there wasn't a leaf left.

Our grandfather, walking a little behind some young men, went to look for our mother but didn't find her. Our grandmother cried with other women and I sang the hymns with them. They brought a little food—some beans—but after two days there was nothing again. Our grandfather used to have three sheep and a cow and a vegetable garden but the bandits had long ago taken the sheep and the cow, because they were hungry, too; and when planting time came our grandfather had no seed to plant.

So they decided—our grandmother did; our grandfather made little noises and rocked from side to side, but she took no notice—we would go away. We children were pleased. We wanted to go away from where our mother wasn't and where we were hungry. We wanted to go where there were no bandits and there was food. We were glad to think there must be such a place; away.

Our grandmother gave her church clothes to someone in exchange for some dried mealies and she boiled them and tied them in a rag. We took them with us when we went and she thought we would get water from the rivers but we didn't come to any river and we got so thirsty we had to turn back. Not all the way to our grandparents' place but to a village where there was a pump. She opened the basket where she carried some clothes and the mealies and she sold her shoes to buy a big plastic container for water. I said, *Gogo*, how will you go to church now even without shoes, but she said we had a long journey and too much to carry. At that village we met other people who were also going away. We joined them because they seemed to know where that was better than we did.

To get there we had to go through the Kruger Park. We knew about the Kruger Park. A kind of whole country of animals—elephants, lions, jackals, hyenas, hippos, crocodiles, all kinds of animals. We had some of them in our own country, before the war (our grandfather remembers; we children weren't born yet) but the bandits kill the elephants and sell their tusks, and the bandits and our soldiers have eaten all the buck. There was a man in our village without legs—a crocodile took them off, in our river; but all the same our country is a country of people, not animals. We knew about the Kruger Park because some of our men used to leave home to work there in the places where white people come to stay and look at the animals.

So we started to go away again. There were women and other children like me who had to carry the small ones on their backs when the women got tired. A man led us into the Kruger Park; are we there yet, are we there yet, I kept asking our grandmother. Not yet, the man said, when she asked him for me. He told us we had to take a long way to get round the fence, which he explained would kill you, roast off your skin the moment you touched it, like the wires high up on poles that give electric light in our towns. I've seen that sign of a head without eyes or skin or hair on an iron box at the mission hospital we used to have before it was blown up.

When I asked the next time, they said we'd been walking in the Kruger Park for an hour. But it looked just like the bush we'd been walking through all day, and we hadn't seen any animals except the monkeys and birds which live around us at home, and a tortoise that, of course, couldn't get away from us. My first-born brother and the other boys brought it to the man so it could be killed and we could cook and eat it. He let it go because he told us we could not make a fire; all the time we were in the Park we must not make a fire because the smoke would show we were there. Police, wardens, would come and send us back where we came from. He said we must move like animals among the animals, away from the roads, away from the white people's camps. And at that moment I heard—I'm sure I was the first to hear—cracking branches and the sound of something parting grasses and I almost squealed because I thought it was the police, wardens—the people he was telling us to look out for—who had found us already. And it was an elephant, and another elephant, and more elephants, big blots of dark moved wherever you looked between the trees. They were curling their trunks round the red leaves of the Mopane trees and stuffing them into their mouths. The babies leant against their mothers. The almost grown-up ones wrestled like my first-born brother with his friends—only they used trunks instead of arms. I was so interested I forgot to be afraid. The man said we should just stand still and be quiet while the elephants passed. They passed very slowly because elephants are too big to need to run from anyone.

The buck ran from us. They jumped so high they seemed to fly. The warthogs stopped dead, when they heard us, and swerved off the way a boy in our village used to zigzag on the bicycle his father had brought back from the mines. We followed the animals to where they drank. When they had gone, we went to their water-holes. We were never thirsty without finding water, but the animals ate, ate all the time. Whenever you saw them they were eating, grass, trees, roots. And there was nothing for us. The mealies were finished. The only food we could eat was what the baboons ate, dry little figs full of ants that grow along the branches of the trees at the rivers. It was hard to be like the animals.

When it was very hot during the day we would find lions lying asleep. They were the color of the grass and we didn't see them at first but the man did, and he led us back and a long way round where they slept. I wanted to lie down like the lions. My little brother was getting thin but he was very heavy. When our grandmother looked for me, to put him on my back, I tried not to see. My first-born brother stopped talking; and when we rested he had to be shaken to get up again, as if he was just like our grandfather, he couldn't hear. I saw flies crawling on our grandmother's face and she didn't brush them off; I was frightened. I picked a palm leaf and chased them.

We walked at night as well as by day. We could see the

fires where the white people were cooking in the camps and we could smell the smoke and the meat. We watched the hyenas with their backs that slope as if they're ashamed, slipping through the bush after the smell. If one turned its head, you saw it had big brown shining eyes like our own, when we looked at each other in the dark. The wind brought voices in our own language from the compounds where the people who work in the camps live. A woman among us wanted to go to them at night and ask them to help us. They can give us the food from the dustbins, she said, she started wailing and our grandmother had to grab her and put a hand over her mouth. The man who led us had told us that we must keep out of the way of our people who worked at the Kruger Park; if they helped us they would lose their work. If they saw us, all they could do was pretend we were not there; they had seen only animals.

Sometimes we stopped to sleep for a little while at night. We slept close together. I don't know which night it was—because we were walking, walking, any time, all the time—we heard the lions very near. Not groaning loudly the way they did far off. Panting, like we do when we run, but it's a different kind of panting: you can hear they're not running, they're waiting, somewhere near. We all rolled closer together, on top of each other, the ones on the edge fighting to get into the middle. I was squashed against a woman who smelled bad because she was afraid but I was glad to hold tight on to her. I prayed to God to make the lions take someone on the edge and go. I shut my eyes not to see the tree from which a lion might jump right into the middle of us, where I was. The man who led us jumped up instead, and beat on the tree with a dead branch. He had taught us never to make a sound but he shouted. He shouted at the lions like a drunk man shouting at nobody, in our village. The lions went away. We heard them groaning, shouting back at him from far off.

We were tired, so tired. My first-born brother and the man had to lift our grandfather from stone to stone where we found places to cross the rivers. Our grandmother is strong but her feet were bleeding. We could not carry the basket on our heads any longer, we couldn't carry anything except my little brother. We left our things under a bush. As long as our bodies get there, our grandmother said. Then we ate some wild fruit we didn't know from home and our stomachs ran. We were in the grass called elephant grass because it is nearly as tall as an elephant, that day we had those pains, and our grandfather couldn't just get down in front of people like my little brother, he went off into the grass to be on his own. We had to keep up, the man who led us always kept telling us, we must catch up, but we asked him to wait for our grandfather.

So everyone waited for our grandfather to catch up. But he didn't. It was the middle of the day; insects were singing in our ears and we couldn't hear him moving through the grass. We couldn't see him because the grass was so high and he was so small. But he must have been somewhere there inside his loose trousers and his shirt that was torn and our grandmother couldn't sew because she had no cotton. We knew he couldn't have gone far because he was weak and slow. We all went to look for him, but in groups, so we too wouldn't be hidden from each other in that grass. It got into our eyes and noses; we called him softly but the noise of the insects must have filled the little space left for hearing in his ears. We looked and looked but we couldn't find him. We stayed in that long grass all night. In my sleep I found him curled round in a place he had tramped down for himself, like the places we'd seen where the buck hide their babies.

When I woke up he still wasn't anywhere. So we looked again, and by now there were paths we'd made by going through the grass many times, it would be easy for him to find us if we couldn't find him. All that day we just sat and waited. Everything is very quiet when the sun is on your head, inside your head, even if you lie, like the animals, under the trees. I lay on my back and saw those ugly birds with hooked beaks and plucked necks flying round and round above us. We had passed them often where they were feeding on the bones of dead animals, nothing was ever left there for us to eat. Round and round, high up and then lower down and then high again. I saw their necks poking to this side and that. Flying round and round. I saw our grandmother, who sat up all the time with my little brother on her lap, was seeing them, too.

In the afternoon the man who led us came to our grandmother and told her the other people must move on. He said, If their children don't eat soon they will die.

Our grandmother said nothing.

I'll bring you water before we go, he told her.

Our grandmother looked at us, me, my first-born brother, and my little brother on her lap. We watched the other people getting up to leave. I didn't believe the grass would be empty, all around us, where they had been. That we would be alone in this place, the Kruger Park, the police or the animals would find us. Tears came out of my eyes and nose onto my hands but our grandmother took no notice. She got up, with her feet apart the way she puts them when she is going to lift firewood, at home in our village, she swung my little brother onto her back, tied him in her cloth—the top of her dress was torn and her big breasts were showing but there was nothing in them for him. She said, Come.

So we left the place with the long grass. Left behind. We went with the others and the man who led us. We started to go away, again.

There's a very big tent, bigger than a church or a school, tied down to the ground. I didn't understand that was what it would be, when we got there, away. I saw a thing like that the time our mother took us to the town because she heard our soldiers were there and she wanted to ask them if they knew where our father was. In that tent, people were praying and singing. This one is blue and white like that one but it's not for praying and singing, we live in it with other people who've come from our country. Sister from the clinic says we're two hundred without counting the babies, and we have new babies, some were born on the way through the Kruger Park.

Inside, even when the sun is bright it's dark and there's a kind of whole village in there. Instead of houses each family has a little place closed off with sacks or cardboard from boxes—whatever we can find—to show the other families it's yours and they shouldn't come in even though there's no door and no windows and no thatch, so that if you're standing up and you're not a small child you can see into everybody's house. Some people have even made paint from ground rocks and drawn designs on the sacks.

Of course, there really is a roof—the tent is the roof, far, high up. It's like a sky. It's like a mountain and we're inside it; through the cracks paths of dust lead down, so thick you think you could climb them. The tent keeps off the rain overhead but the water comes in at the sides and in the little streets between our places—you can only move along them one person at a time—the small kids like my little brother play in the mud. You have to step over them. My little brother doesn't play. Our grand-mother takes him to the clinic when the doctor comes on Mondays. Sister says there's something wrong with his head, she thinks it's because we didn't have enough food at home. Because of the war. Because our father wasn't there. And then because he was so hungry in the Kruger Park. He likes just to lie about on our grandmother all day, on her lap or against her somewhere, and he looks at us and looks at us. He wants to ask something but you can see he can't. If I tickle him he may just smile. The clinic gives us special powder to make into porridge for him and perhaps one day he'll be all right.

When we arrived we were like him—my first-born brother and I. I can hardly remember. The people who live in the village near the tent took us to the clinic, it's where you have to sign that you've come—away, through the Kruger Park. We sat on the grass and everything was muddled. One Sister was pretty with her hair straight-ened and beautiful high-heeled shoes and she brought us the special powder. She said we must mix it with water and drink it slowly. We tore the packets open with our teeth and licked it all up, it stuck round my mouth and I sucked it from my lips and fingers. Some other children who had walked with us vomited. But I only felt everything in my belly moving, the stuff going down and around like a snake, and hiccups hurt me. Another Sister called us to stand in line on the verandah of the clinic but we couldn't. We sat all over the place there, falling against each other; the Sisters helped each of us up by the arm and then stuck a needle in it. Other needles drew our blood into tiny bottles. This was against sickness, but I didn't understand, every time my eyes dropped closed I thought I was walking, the grass was long, I saw the elephants, I didn't know we were away.

But our grandmother was still strong, she could still stand up, she knows how to write and she signed for us. Our grandmother got us this place in the tent against one of the sides, it's the best kind of place there because although the rain comes in, we can lift the flap when the weather is good and then the sun shines on us, the smells in the tent go out. Our grandmother knows a woman here who showed her where there is good grass for sleeping mats, and our grandmother made some for us. Once every month the food truck comes to the clinic. Our grandmother takes along one of the cards she signed and when it has been punched we get a sack of mealie meal. There are wheelbarrows to take it back to the tent; my first-born brother does this for her and then he and the other boys have races, steering the empty wheelbarrows back to the clinic. Sometimes he's lucky and a man who's bought beer in the village gives him money to deliver it—though that's not allowed, you're supposed to take that wheelbarrow straight back to the Sisters. He buys a cold drink and shares it with me if I catch him. On another day, every month, the church leaves a pile of old clothes in the clinic yard. Our grandmother has another card to get punched, and then we can choose something: I have two dresses, two pants and a jersey, so I can go to school.

The people in the village have let us join their school. I was surprised to find they speak our language; our grandmother told me, That's why they allow us to stay on their land. Long ago, in the time of our fathers, there was no fence that kills you, there was no Kruger Park between them and us, we were the same people under our own king, right from our village we left to this place we've come to.

Now that we've been in the tent so long—I have turned eleven and my little brother is nearly three although he is so small, only his head is big, he's not come right in it yet—some people have dug up the bare ground around the tent and planted beans and mealies and cabbage. The old men weave branches to put up fences round their gardens. No one is allowed to look for work in the towns but some of the women have found work in the village and can buy things. Our grandmother, because she's still strong, finds work where people are building houses—in this village the people build nice houses with bricks and cement, not mud like we used to have at our home. Our grandmother carries bricks for these people and fetches baskets of stones on her head. And so she has money to buy sugar and tea and milk and soap. The store gave her a calendar she has hung up on our flap of the tent. I am clever at school and she collected advertising paper people throw away outside the store and covered my schoolbooks with it. She makes my first-born brother and me do our homework every afternoon before it gets dark because there is no room except to lie down, close together, just as we did in the Kruger Park, in our place in the tent, and candles are expensive. Our grandmother hasn't been able to buy herself a pair of shoes for church yet, but she has bought black school shoes and polish to clean them with for my first-born brother and me. Every morning, when people are getting up in the tent, the babies are crying, people are pushing each other at the taps outside and some children are already pulling the crusts of porridge off the pots we ate from last night, my first-born brother and I clean our shoes. Our grandmother makes us sit on our mats with our legs straight out so she can look carefully at our shoes to make sure we have done it properly. No other children in the tent have real school shoes. When we three look at them it's as if we are in a real house again, with no war, no away.

Some white people came to take photographs of our people living in the tent—they said they were making a film, I've never seen what that is though I know about it. A white woman squeezed into our space and asked our grandmother questions which were told to us in our language by someone who understands the white woman's.

How long have you been living like this?

She means here? our grandmother said. In this tent, two years and one month.

And what do you hope for the future?

Nothing. I'm here.

But for your children?

I want them to learn so that they can get good jobs and money.

Do you hope to go back to Mozambique—to your own country?

I will not go back.

But when the war is over—you won't be allowed to stay here. Don't you want to go home?

I didn't think our grandmother wanted to speak again. I didn't think she was going to answer the white woman. The white woman put her head on one side and smiled at us.

Our grandmother looked away from her and spoke— There is nothing. No home.

Why does our grandmother say that? Why? I'll go back. I'll go back through that Kruger Park. After the war, if there are no bandits any more, our mother may be waiting for us. And maybe when we left our grandfather, he was only left behind, he found his way somehow, slowly, through the Kruger Park, and he'll be there. They'll be home, and I'll remember them.

Glossary

amaKula: (Zulu, from English *coolie* or Tamil/Telegu *kūli* "hired person") unskilled laborers, derogatory.

Antjie die Boerin: (Afrikaans) Antjie the country woman, farmer.

assegai: a slender hardwood spear.

baas: (Afrikaans) boss, master.

bakkie: (Afrikaans) pick-up truck.

biltong: strips of dried meat.

bioscope: cinema, an early film projector.

boer: (Afrikaans) farmer; a rural Afrikaner; a derogatory name for Afrikaners (when used by non-Afrikaners).

bogadi: (Tswana, Sotho) bride price.

bowser boy: service station attendant.

bri-bri, mntanam, uyagula!: (or probably *mntanam uyakhula,* Xhosa) Wow, my child, you are growing!

bundu: (South African English, possibly from Shona) boondocks, wilds.

dagga: (Afrikaans from Khoikhoi *dachab*) marijuana.

doek: (Afrikaans) headscarf, as worn by so many African women.

doppers: (Afrikaans) members of the Dutch Reformed Church.

gogo: grandmother

haaikona: (from Zulu *hayi khona*) an emphatic negative; certainly not! Oh no!

hajji: (from Arabic) one who has made the pilgrimage to
    Mecca.

hau: (from Zulu and Xhosa *Hawu!*) an interjection of pained
    surprise, disappointment, sorrow; Oh no! Oh dear! What
    have you done!

Hau, unjani ukubeka, iphi wena hamba? (perhaps *Hawu,
    unjani? Ubheka phi?* Zulu) Gosh, how are you? Where are
    you headed?

hayi: (Xhosa, Zulu) no!; an exclamation of surprise.

hei ngoana 'rona: (Sothern Sotho) hey! My child, my brother.

hela batho: (Southern Sotho) good gracious.

hendsopper: (generally *henshopper;* Afrikaans) derogatory for
    Afrikaners who surrendered to the British; literally hands-
    upper.

herrenvolk: (German) master race.

he wena! Ke eng tse, hee: (Southern Sotho) hey, you! What are
    these, then?

hijaars: (or *hejab*; Arabic) head covering worn by Muslim women.

hire-purchase: installment plan.

hottentots: name used formerly by the Dutch to describe
    the native inhabitants of the Cape, now referred to as
    Khoekhoe.

huwii: an expression of surprise, oh!

imbongi: (Zulu, Xhosa) praise poet.

in' indaba: (probably *Yin 'indaba*; Zulu) What is the matter?

kaffir: (from Arabic "nonbeliever") offensive term for a black
    person.

kappie: (Afrikaans) bonnet.

kaross: cloak or rug made of skins.

Ke teng. Wena?: (Southern Sotho) I'm fine. And how about
    you?

kêrels: (Dutch) lads, fellows, chaps.

kgotla: (Sotho, Tswana) place of assembly, court.

kierie: knobkerrie or wooden club.

klap: (South African English, from Afrikaans) slap, snap.

klawerjas: (usually *klaberjas/klabberjas*; Afrikaans) popular card game.

kloof: (Afrikaans) a gorge or a narrow pass between mountains.

koekies: (Afrikaans) small cake.

koeksisters: (Afrikaans) twisted or plaited traditional pastries.

kona!: (or *Nyikhona, Zulu*) I'm fine.

koppie: (Afrikaans) a hill on the African veld, or grassland.

kraal: (Afrikaans from Portuguese) corral, animal fold, usually refers to a traditional African village.

krot: (Afrikaans) hovel.

lobola: (from Xhosa, Zulu) bride price.

locations: townships or designated black/African residential areas.

maar nie vir daardie Engelse kaffir nie: (Afrikaans) but not for that English kaffir.

mealies: corn, maize.

miltsiek: (Afrikaans) anthrax, a virulent disease of the blood.

moshiman'o: (Tswana) this boy.

nagmaal: (Afrikaans) communion in the Dutch Reformed Church.

'nooi': (Afrikaans) a submissive term of address used by black people with white women. The female equivalent of *baas*.

O kae?: (Southern Sotho) how are you?

oom: (Afrikaans) uncle, term of respect for an older male.

outjie: (Afrikaans) fellow, chap.

ox-riem: (Afrikaans) leather strap used for oxen.

poort: (Afrikaans) door; also a steep narrow mountain pass.

riempies-bank: (Afrikaans) a bench with the seat made from criss-crossed strips of hide.

robot: traffic light.

rooineks: (Afrikaans) derogatory term for British; literally rednecks.

sasarties: (generally *sosaties*; Afrikaans) cubes of grilled meat on a skewer, kebab.

Sawubona, Poobal; unjani?: (Zulu) Hello, Poobal, how are you?

sjambok: (Afrikaans) a heavy whip.

skeis: (Afrikaans) The pin between two oxen yokes, one for each animal.

skollies: (Afrikaans) hoodlums, gang members.

sloot: (Dutch) ditch.

titihoya: (from Zulu *ititihoye*) black-winged plover.

tsotsis: (derived from zoot suit) hoodlums.

uitlander: (Afrikaans) outlander; a foreigner.

veld: (Afrikaans) grassland, often mixed with shrubs and trees.

veldkornet: (Afrikaans) field cornet; a military rank.

veldschoens: (Afrikaans) shoes or ankle boots made of rough leather.

veldskoens: see veldschoens.

vierkleur: (Afrikaans "four colors") the flag of the old Transvaal Republic.

voetsek: (Afrikaans) get lost, bug off.

voorkamer: (Afrikaans) forechamber, front room.

Waar vanaf kom julle?: (Afrikaans) Where do you [plural] come from?

What is jy?: (Afrikaans) What are you?

Wat! Nie "Skilpadfontein baas" nie?: (Afrikaans) What! Not "Skilpadfontein, boss"?

witdoeke: (Afrikaans) vigilantes, specifically groups of men opposing squatters and leftist activists in the 1970s and 1980s, identified by their white scarves.

Woonjani, we Dumi?: (or *Unjani, we Dumi?* Zulu) How are you, Dumi?

woza weekend: (Zulu) roll-on (or come) weekend

ISABEL BALSEIRO is the Alexander and Adelaide Hixon Professor of Humanities at Harvey Mudd College, in Claremont, California. Several times a research associate at the Centre for African Studies, University of Cape Town, her publications on South Africa include *To Change Reels: Film and Film Culture in South Africa* and the anthology *Running Towards Us: New Writing from South Africa*.

TOBIAS HECHT is the author of *At Home in the Street: Street Children of Northeast Brazil*, which won the Margaret Mead Award, and *After Life: An Ethnographic Novel*. One of his short stories won second prize in Spain's Hucha de Oro, which carries the world's largest prize for a single piece of short fiction. An independent scholar, writer, and translator, he received his Ph.D. from Cambridge. His current writing concerns denialism in relation to the AIDS epidemic in South Africa.